Full Throttle

by

Sir Henry ("Tim") Birkin, Bt.

foreword by

The Rt. Hon. THE EARL HOWE P.C., C.B.E., V.D.

Clink Street

Published by Clink Street Publishing 2021

First edition.

Full Throttle was first published in 1932 by G.T. Foulis & Co., Ltd

This new Daredevil Books edition is published in association with Clink Street Publishing, London and follows the text of the first book edition with minor emendations and a revised selection of photographs.

www.daredevilbooks.co.uk

ISBN:
978-1-913568-69-6 - paperback
978-1-913568-70-2 - ebook

Contents

THIS BOOK IS DEDICATED TO
ALL SCHOOLBOYS

Sir Henry Ralph Stanley "Tim" Birkin, 3rd Baronet
26 July 1896 – 22 June 1933

Acknowledgments

I am deeply grateful to my uncle, who lent me five pounds to build a car at the age of sixteen, and to the soap-box which was its body. I am also grateful to my unwearying secretary, who has helped me in my races as much as in the throes of composition; to Mr. Adams, who has collected my Press cuttings, a labour at which Hercules would have trembled; to those who corrected my illegible handwriting, my spelling, and my punctuation mistakes; to several people who were dishonest enough to say they liked the book, and several more who were honest enough to say they did not, and finally to Lord Howe for the favour of his Foreword, which should sell more copies than the whole of the rest of the book.

My attention having been called to the fact that certain criticisms of the Brooklands Track made in this Book may be construed as a reflection upon the Proprietors of the Track and the Brooklands Automobile Racing Club of which I am a member, in their conduct of the premises, I wish unreservedly to state that such was never my intention, and that if in my advocacy of what I believe to be a matter of supreme importance to the future of British prestige in the motor world I have in any way exceeded the bounds of fair and reasonable comment, I unreservedly withdraw such statements and tender my apologies for the publication thereof. I am assured and fully accept the statement that there have been no fatalities at Brooklands due to the condition of the track and I am aware of the stringent regulations laid down by the Club to prevent accidents.

HENRY R. S. BIRKIN,
1st Dec., 1932.

Introduction

Apart from a few forays in 1921 on a DFP (the marque first tuned and raced by W.O.Bentley), Birkin's racing career lasted just seven seasons, from 1927 to 1933. In that time he oversaw the development of the spectacular, but flawed, "Blower" supercharged 4½-litre Bentley; won the 24 Hours of Le Mans twice; and broke the Brooklands Outer Circuit lap record with his supercharged single-seater Bentley. He also produced some heroic non-winning performances, of which the greatest must have been his second place – in a field otherwise composed of specialist racing machinery – in his four-seat "Blower" 4½, at the Pau Grand Prix in 1930.

Full Throttle was originally published in 1932, when Birkin was at the height of his driving success and celebrity standing, but with less than a year of his life remaining. Nearly 90 years later, we have the benefit of hindsight in looking at his whole career, and we can also look more at his early and private lives – subjects which he pointedly declined to cover in the book. So we know that he was the elder son of a Baronet, born in 1896, and that in World War 1 he served with the 108th (Norfolk & Suffolk Yeomanry)

Field Brigade in Palestine, and in the Royal Flying Corps, attaining the rank of Captain. The family's business was in lace, in Nottingham, but Birkin favoured Norfolk, where he kept his 30ft launch *Ida* and where (at Blakeney) he is buried.

We know that he married in 1921, had two daughters and was divorced in 1928 – but that without a son as heir his title passed to his uncle's side of the family. Perhaps the most important woman in his life, however, was the Hon Dorothy Paget, who from 1928 funded Birkin's development and racing of the supercharged Bentley, and even after she withdrew her support for this venture in 1930 retained ownership of the famous single-seater for him to race.

When Earl Howe wrote his foreword to the first edition of *Full Throttle,* he did so without the advantage that we do, of having read the book! So he perhaps was unaware that – despite the implication in Birkin's Acknowledgements, expressing gratitude to "…those who corrected my illegible handwriting, my spelling and my punctuation mistakes…" – it wasn't really Birkin's work. The book was, in fact, ghost-written in three weeks flat by a young student with no previous experience of authorship, Michael Burn, later to be a prisoner of war, poet, playwright and correspondent to *The Times.*

Howe would also have been unaware of the furore which would greet the book's publication, when the Brooklands Estate Company sued Birkin for libel on account of his criticism of the track over more than three pages, including describing it as "…without exception, the most out-of-date, inadequate and dangerous track in the world." Birkin was forced to issue a signed statement to be slipped into subsequent copies of the book, stating: "My attention having been called to the fact that certain criticisms of the Brooklands track made in this book may be construed as a reflection upon the proprietors of the track, and the Brooklands Automobile Racing Club, in their conduct of the premises, I wish unreservedly to state that such was never my intention, I unreservedly withdraw such statements and tender my apologies for the publication of them". Interestingly, the offending wording was not expunged from later editions, such as my own copy from 1943, which – if it ever contained it – shows no evidence of the apology.

Whatever the legal niceties, motor racing in Birkin's era – whether at Brooklands or elsewhere – was a dangerous game, and an immensely physically demanding one, too. Those of us who are privileged to drive their wonderful machines in the modern era know something of the heavy controls, harsh suspension, comparative lack of roadholding and braking, and recalcitrant unsychronised gearboxes faced by Birkin and his contemporaries. We, however, have it easy: we drive on smooth tracks; away from the very few purpose-built circuits like Brooklands, Montlhéry and Monza, they raced on often unpaved public roads, facing heat, dust, flying stones and rutted surfaces. Where we have run-off areas and safety barriers, they faced unprotected roadside walls, ditches and telegraph poles. Without the benefits of modern tyre technology, they lived with the constant risk of tyres disintegrating, and they faced all this without the comfort of seatbelts, rollcages, deformable crash structures or fireproof clothing.

If Birkin were to revisit his book in the 21st century, one aspect of it that he would undoubtedly be pleased to remove would be his trenchant criticism of the British motor-racing establishment and manufacturers over the country's lack of world-class racing cars, teams and circuits. With the majority of Formula One teams resident in Britain, along with world-leading suppliers to them and other racing categories and some of the world's best circuits, things have changed for the better. But Birkin's analyses of what makes a good driver and of winning race-craft remain as valid as ever, even if the world in which he formed those views has disappeared.

Allan Winn is a Vice-President of Brooklands Museum, where he was for 15 years the Director and CEO. A New Zealander by birth, he holds a degree in Mechanical Engineering and Diploma in Journalism: his first career in business and technical magazines culminated as Editor and then Publisher of Flight International. He is Chairman of Aviation Heritage UK, a Vice-President of the National Transport Trust, Honorary Vice-President of the Association of Heritage Engineers and a former Chairman of the Aviation Club UK. A Fellow of the Royal Aeronautical Society he is a lifelong classic and vintage motorist and served for 17 years on the Committee of the Vintage Sports Car Club. He has owned and used his 1929 3-Litre Bentley since 1985.

Original Foreword by The Rt. Hon. The Earl Howe, P.C., C.B.E., V.D.

I feel very much honoured that I should have been invited to write a Foreword in the book which Sir Henry Birkin is compiling upon his experiences in motor racing.

At the moment of writing I have not had an opportunity of seeing his book and have, therefore, no knowledge of what the keen student of motor racing will find in it, but if it is, as I imagine it will be, a complete record of his experiences, it will be a record of gallant adventure and endeavour by one of the finest sportsmen and most brilliant drivers that this or any other country has ever produced.

In motor-car racing, at any rate in this country, there are two different kinds of drivers. Firstly, the driver who is at his best on the road; secondly, the driver who specialises on the track.

I have always looked upon Tim Birkin as belonging very definitely to the first category, gallant though his performances have been with the great single seater Bentley, and with reference to the latter,

I believe it is true to say he has completed over fifty laps at Brooklands with that car, at 135 m.p.h. or more, and now holds the Brooklands Lap Record of 137.89 m.p.h.

As one who has himself endeavoured to get round the Brooklands Track at fairly high speed, I am in a better position than most people who have not had this opportunity, to appreciate the terrific nature of the undertaking.

To take a very fast car round the Brooklands Track at high speed requires the greatest courage and an iron nerve, but great as are the qualities required for competing on the track, I have always been of the opinion that a road race is a far more supreme test of the individual, as in addition to all the pluck required to compete upon the track, a far higher standard of skill and of good judgment is required on the road.

Sir Henry Birkin has hardly ever competed in a road race without putting up a remarkable performance. Though I was not lucky enough to compete in either event, from the remarks which I have heard Continental drivers make with regard to Tim's prowess, I am perfectly certain that two performances which he put up on the road stand out in particular. One was the Grand Prix de Pau, in 1930, when he drove a 4 litre Bentley with a four-seater body against some of the pick of the Continental drivers in purely racing cars. He came in second after a drive which was hair-raising in character, and which no doubt he will describe in his book. The comment usually made by the greatest of Continental drivers is that nothing finer has ever been done by anybody, and that if he had started off a little quicker he would actually have won the race.

The other performance was when partnered by that brilliant driver, the Hon. Brian Lewis. He came in fourth in the Belgian Grand Prix in 1931, driving a Sports Type Alfa-Romeo with a four-seater body against the very pick of the Continental drivers equipped with the very latest type of Grand Prix racing machines.

Both these performances, in my judgment, were thoroughly characteristic of the man and the brilliant sportsman that Tim Birkin is, in the minds of those who know him.

Perhaps I may be forgiven if I add a word with reference to motor racing in general.

I have often been asked, "What is the good of motor racing?" The shortest answer that I can give is that in common with all other forms of competition, it plays its part in developing the breed. The motor-car of to-day and its accessories, whether a public service or a private vehicle, would never have reached the pitch of development which it has had it not been for the supreme test to which it has been put, and the important lessons thereby learned in motor racing.

Few people realise the tremendous advances which motor racing has brought about, even during the past year, in the products of the great Continental factories, and this progress still continues.

Power weight ratios, previously thought to be quite unattainable, have been used with outstanding success, and the next few years will see improvements made in racing cars with front-wheel drive, four-wheel drive, pre-selector devices, electrical welding, etc., to mention only a few; while the tyre manufacturers have to deal with a problem of increasing difficulty as the performance goes up.

From the driver it requires a degree of physical fitness unsurpassed by other forms of sport, a combination of courage, cool judgment and nerve, which is so entirely exemplified in the personality of Sir Henry Birkin. In addition, he brings to his aid a technical knowledge of the highest order.

Few of us in England realise the enormous importance attached to motor racing on the Continent. During the months of May, June, July and August, last year there were no less than forty-five motor races of one sort and another in Italy alone, in addition to the large number of events taking place during the same period in France, Germany, Belgium, etc.

Success in the big Continental events carries great international prestige, and is looked upon as being a great advertisement for the industries of the countries concerned; so much so that it is common knowledge that in some countries the governments concerned have considered it worthwhile to render assistance to the competing firms, either directly or indirectly. This being so, one cannot help feeling that it is a very great pity that some of the English firms cannot make greater efforts to compete either individually or collectively. When the day comes, as I feel sure it will, when some of the leaders of the English firms will be prepared to enter into this world of intensive competition, I am quite certain that they will find Sir Henry Birkin in particular and all his colleagues of the British Racing World will be ready to place the whole of their technical knowledge and experience at their disposal, in order to do everything possible to ensure success for England.

Reproduced with the kind permission of
Frederick Curzon, 7th Earl Howe

— CHAPTER I —

A Car

When I began to write this book, I realised at once that someone was going to be disappointed. It was a disheartening first conclusion; but, inevitably, either the expert would be dissatisfied, finding too little technical detail, too little attention to the evolution of certain cars, or the amateur, finding too much. The problem could not be shelved, and after due thought and endless regrets, I decided to sacrifice the expert. At the end of this, the first paragraph, I see one whole contingent of my readers rueing the hour they ever bought the book, or, more accurately, borrowed it from their library. But I had my reasons for this decision.

Many of them will be members of the great ordinary-car-owning public, interested to hear about an aspect of motoring in which they have no active concern. They will like to read of the thrills they enjoy watching, but have no desire to experience. They are bored by a car's inside, which they generally prefer should remain a complete stranger to them, and regard on many occasions as a definite enemy. I feel, too, that most experts' knowledge of technicalities is greater than my own, and therefore cannot be benefited by anything I may say on the matter.

It would be idle to apologise for my literary style, because there is no one so exacting as to think that the hand, used for years to the steering wheel, will have a similar good fortune with the pen. I am the last person to expect Edith Sitwell, in however fast a car, to win the Double Twelve at Brooklands, or Bernard Shaw the Le Mans Endurance Prize, and I have a right to claim the same indulgence for myself.

Moreover I am indebted for much of my material to old Press cuttings, and as the book has been written in a considerable hurry, I have not been able to elude the influence of their style: nouns seem linked inseparably with one particular adjective, and phrases stream forth, however keenly I resist them.

Cars never seem to do anything but "roar through the night," or "thunder round the track," while the tone of a supercharger is standardised as a "whine." There is no such thing as an exciting race; it is "a thrilling tussle for supremacy," and a fine track is "a gruelling test of nerves and efficiency." This is perhaps regrettable, though it may be just that exaggerated words should be used for the sport I consider the greatest in the world; and perhaps the excitement caused by a struggle between magnificent cars leaves one gasping for more poetic language. So please do not imagine, if any account of such-

and-such a race leaves you cold, that it is from lack of enthusiasm on my part; put it down to an unfortunate education that did not teach me my own tongue better. For I have got more excitement out of a few minutes in a car than most people out of a lifetime, and I know they could do the same if they chose. Motor racing holds such a variety of thrills, and such a multitude of difficulties beset it, that any other sport pales utterly by comparison.

This is the opinion I have formed in a very little while; it has prompted every one of the following pages, and now that I have finished, I see no cause to modify it. But should anyone be moved after reading of the immense speeds attained in the races here related to try things with their own conveyances of which they are not capable, I have added a few words of simple warning: I do not want to have laid at my door catastrophes caused by inspired spinsters driving at 50 m.p.h. down Piccadilly, or by owners who ruined their cars for an extra two or three miles. Just as there are times – though I go to prison for saying so – when it is permissible to go "flat-out" on main thoroughfares, so there are corners in the very fastest events, such as the Dundonald hairpin in the T.T., which can only be taken at 15 m.p.h. or less.

My first difficulty was the choice of a title dramatic enough for its theme, and the one that stands was only decided on after many beautiful, witty and imbecile suggestions. "Racing Demon" was at first popular. It was not meant to insinuate anything fiendish or unpleasant in the character of those who race; but those who know about cards will remember that it is the name of a game of chance. Motor racing is a game of chance; there is a huge preponderance of skill in it, but a time comes – either someone in front has crashed or something blows across the track, or one of the thousand hideous unforeseen things happens – when only Fate can decide between safety and disaster. Those who do not consider Chance, do not deserve to be favoured by her.

The name "Demon" too, is at times appropriate to a car; at night especially, it is a terrifying and almost unearthly sight, when the headlights come from afar sweeping round a corner, then abruptly racing straight for you like the eyes of a demon, and the murmur of the engine grows out of silence into that sharp and deafening roar, to die quickly away as more and more come hot upon its heels.

A title which received a good many votes was "Spinning Wheels" and might have looked well on the jacket with a suitable design, but it was abandoned, being thought likely to give the impression that the book was about the cotton industry.

I have dedicated the book, as you see, to schoolboys all over the world, partly, a piece of publishers' diplomacy, to make the schoolboys' mothers buy it for the schoolboys' Christmas present, and partly out of a genuine gratitude. On the day of a big race, I have never been without some mascot of heather, or a black cat, sent from this quarter, and I am most sensible of the interest taken. Carraciola, on returning from his great victory at Belfast, was more struck he said, by the enthusiasm and knowledge of the young than by anything else. It is an excellent thing and I recommend most parents, in search of technical information, to ask for it first from their children.

In most books dealing with motor racing that I have read, much space at the beginning is devoted to early life, and the gradual birth of a passion for speed. There are touching stories about money saved up to buy toy cars, which are then subjected to a miniature Brooklands round the nursery floor, and innocent reminiscences of "my first crash," which takes place on the garden path, are woven into charming anecdotes. Slowly adolescence brings a realisation that the hero's element is the track, that he was born for that alone, and, come what may, he will fulfil that purpose. Gallant resolve! But no, a father's will interposes: "Into an office you go, my would-be champion."

The subsequent crisis is variously treated. In novels he runs away, or takes somebody's place in a big event – presumably while the whole of the pit has its back turned – and after a magnificent fight, wins for England, receiving a large cheque and a permanent job to the tune of "God Save the King." In real life, he gets taken on at a garage, and works his way up from the bottom. However told, it is extremely edifying, and a fashion I have no intention of following. To those who would like to have heard of me poring over motor books when I should have been learning my catechism, or breaking out of school to go to Brooklands instead of Ascot, I offer my deepest apologies; my mind is lit with no such memories, nor shall my book be. I do not believe it will make much difference, because my early youth and the habits of my family can have next to no interest for the public. If I blamed anything for my devotion to cars and subsequent rushing into print, it would be something blamed already for so many troubles, that one more can make no odds - the war.

I was in the Air Force, and, when Armistice came, found the view of my future life, as I then beheld it, a very dull and confined one. It was bounded by the four walls of an office, which afforded none of the excitements of the career I was leaving. Each day would seem more vapid and tedious than the last, and I thoroughly disliked the outlook. An explanation of this emotion, that preferred a state of unrest to one of rest, is difficult after fourteen years, especially to a generation whose memories of war are vague. But there were at the time many in sympathy with it, who were only prevented from yielding to it by economic barriers, and found the first period of sedentary business, into which they were forced, intolerably empty. I was lucky enough to have the money to look round for an occupation, and not accept the first that offered, and of all that I considered, motor racing provided the energy, adventures and risks most like those of the battlefield. It had, moreover, the promise of a great future and there was the same chance of unexpected disaster, the same need for perfect nerves, with a presence of mind that must never desert you, the same exhilaration of living in the shadow of a death that often came so suddenly and gloriously, that it seemed to have no shadow. There was, besides, the peculiar delight of being responsible for your own calamities, since, once off the mark, you were at liberty to take risks or avoid them as you pleased, a state of independence few individuals enjoyed in the war. All your attention, the possibility of a crash over the banking, alternating with a glorious run at high speed and nothing to hinder, all the thrills and sinking at heart, are concentrated into a few yards of road, and a strip of metal, which is as fine an accomplishment as anything in modern times. In it are packed all the newest ingenuities that the most brilliant minds have conceived, slight changes that mean a small precious increase in speed, and minute devices guarding against the most unexpected catastrophes. It is evolved by the hand of man out of his brain, to be used by him as a means to further evolutions, higher speeds, and greater security and it is tested, not in the close atmosphere of a laboratory, unknown to anybody, but in the open country over clear stretches of road and round right-angle corners, between avenues of excited spectators. The praise of racing cars can best be sung by those who live with them; to these, the finished product is not a mere case of metal, with nuts and gadgets inside, but the offspring of the union of many minds, each one of which is represented in a particular part. It is the climax of years of investigation and disappointment and not being contented with success. There is no machine of equal importance that man has brought nearer both practical and apparent perfection.

When finally it is wheeled from the workshop by its jealous makers, and the lucky driver feels the new life suddenly throbbing through all its members, the cheers of the crowd, impressed only by a beautiful appearance and terrific speed, take on a deeper meaning. God created man in His own image, and that was considered the noblest of all creations. Now man is creating something, the regularity and concord of whose working are beginning to rival his own. Each part of a racing car has its own function, which it has to perform without fail and co-ordinate with all the other parts without fail, so that efficiency in one department need not be sacrificed to efficiency in another, and speed may be consistent with endurance. It is the same with a man; and, as in a man, so in a car, perfect combination of all the members is the aim. It becomes a thing of latent power, only waiting for a touch of the foot to spring into action, and to give this is the privilege of the driver. With one movement he can stop it completely, with another inspire it to attack all records, steadily increasing its speed, until sometimes in its exuberance it runs away from him, or he is unable to control it, and both are destroyed.

I wish I had the words to utter my belief that a car has a life of its own, or impart a little of its keenness and power. What I have said is unconvincing, while to the schoolmaster who observed, "I can see no beauty whatever in a racing car," I am afraid I have nothing to say at all.

Surely it is not surprising, when the time comes for testing these wonderful machines, that the men who have spent most of their life in making them should then be prepared to risk losing it entirely. 1 regret that here, and in many oilier passages, I shall lay myself open to the odious charge of trumpet-blowing, but I have gone on this principle, that either I succeed in a race, or I do not. If I do not, I am very glad that other men should have from the public the praise they always commanded from their friends; and if I do, I look to the judgments of spectators, thank my stars, and give credit to the car that made victory possible. I want no special merit attached to my own races, except that they enable me to give a more intimate account of the event than an onlooker could; and if my trumpet is too loud, I apologise sincerely for an error I have tried to avoid.

But there is no need to stint my praise of racing motorists in general. I have no patience whatever with people who condemn them for hot-headed fools, and stamp their performances as an ebullition of useless bravado. That is the criticism of men who, having since youth made no progress except backwards themselves, resent and even refuse to recognise it in others. Every big motor race is a means of further discovery, and every racer is working, not for himself, not even entirely for his firm, but for the whole industry of his country, and the increase of speed, comfort and endurance in motor transport. His appeal to the public should be, and is becoming, greater every year, for, by the dangers he incurs comes the possibility of an extra few miles in the car they buy, or an extra year on its duration. In this way he benefits the very people whose malice stigmatises his dare-devilry as wasted. In the service of the public he courts risks and goes in peril of his life. The Press cuttings of big races are full of his heroism, of men eager to carry on despite appalling burns and injuries, deliberately continuing in pain, when there was a chance of honourable surrender, and exercising all their powers of body and mind to defeat accident. They bind up their wings with straps, climb along the bonnet when travelling at great speed, remove mudguards, and even stop gaps with wads of chewing gum; they go round corners on two wheels, fly through the air for fractions of a second, and miss trees, lakes, ditches, hedges and other cars by less than inches. They enjoy it enthusiastically themselves, as I do, preferring this sport to every other, and contributing to it their experience, with all the youth and courage in their blood, sometimes they fail and are soon forgotten, unless they had time to establish a great international reputation. *Vixere fortes ante Agamemnona* – there have been, before and after Segrave, many first-class drivers who remained unknown to the majority and let others reap their harvest. Some were killed in the service of civilisation, thereby giving the journalists some fine copy, and increasing the sales of the next day's newspapers. Others broke records, enjoyed a brief spell of floodlighting, and then watched them broken again a few days later. Others, after designing, helping in and supervising the construction of their own car, drove it proudly before admiring crowds to the threshold of a great victory, happy that the product of their labours was about to succeed, and then, suddenly, towards the end, saw it hidden in a sheet of flames and utterly destroyed. This was Malcolm Campbell's experience with his Bugatti at Ulster in 1928; the Press made a fine story out of it, and there were some good photographs.

Much, indeed, might deter a man from venturing a precious car in a dangerous race but, while the certainty that the car cannot do itself justice might cause its withdrawal, mere fright has no sort of influence. A driver is as likely to scratch his car because he is frightened as he is to throw a banana skin in his opponent's path, and the odds against that happening are further witness to his good character. I believe – God forbid I should spread a whisper of scandal – but I believe that there exist in horse-racing examples of what may be termed hanky-panky, that there have been occasions, rare perhaps, but still occasions, when one horse has won a race through the skill of another horse's jockey, and even when some horses have failed to run in their race at all. The opportunities for hanky-panky with motors are far greater than with horses, but the examples correspondingly fewer. They might indeed be more, were motor racing a matter of bitter rivalry between individuals and firms, not a friendly, if thrilling, competition for a common cause. Perhaps this absence of intrigue and trickery is one of the reasons that cars are not yet so installed in the hearts of the people as horses; for this is the case, though horses are the luxury of the few, and cars of the many. In time the incongruity will right itself; while horses keep their appeal by an antiquarian charm, increasing yearly, and their jockeys retain popular affection by a knavish aspect and a suspicion of notoriety, cars are developing an equal, but different kind of attraction. The finer subtleties of their beauty are valued higher. There is something more enthralling about the labour out of which they are created, and their improvements, tested in the world's most hazardous races, begin to be admired by those they benefit, while their drivers atone more than amply for lack of conspiracy, by bravery and resource.

Every year the attendance at big motor races swells; and the time is not very far distant when the world will make Belfast a goal as sought after as Epsom or Aintree. The Turf has been from time immemorial the pastime of the aristocracy, but even that most conservative body is turning its eye-glass elsewhere, and, though in the pits there is but one specimen of

Privy Councillor, many is the overall beneath which the blue blood beats.

Some people will criticise my neglect of history, because I have not gone back to the beginnings out of which the present machines and contests were evolved, and left all the wealth of humour and interest in early racing unevoked. But most of the humour is well known, while pictures of vehicles so constructed, that their driver was boiled from the waist down and frozen from the waist up, no longer amuse with their old quaintness. I have not even included a photograph of King Edward in the first automobile, observing as marked a reticence about their youth as about my own. I have but one distant recollection with which to entertain you. When I first started active interest, I was reading a novel about Mr. Sherlock Holmes, who found occasion, in pursuit of some fugitive scoundrel, to make use of a car. There ensues the most dramatic description of the chase, which arrested my eye for anything fast or exciting; in and out of side streets it went, along river banks, on the edge of precipices, until I was breathless from following. Gasping, I turned the page, to find this sentence, and one of my bitterest disillusions: "We were now travelling along the high road at the terrific pace of *25 Miles an Hour!*" . . . Since then I have lost interest in the infancy of speed.

But I suppose its first great exponent was one, whose very existence is in question, who partook in a race where he was the only competitor, and achieved a performance more perilous than has ever been approached since. His name was Phaethon, and he was one of the many sons for whom Apollo was at fault. One fine day, the myth says, he borrowed his father's car, which was, of course, the chariot of the sun, and set out to drive it round its usual course from east to west. He drove it faster than it had ever been driven before, at well over a million miles an hour, until, like most cars, quick to resent an unskilled hand, it got out of control and entered into a terrible skid. This brought it so close to the earth that inhabitants of the nearest country, which happened to be Africa, were severely scorched, and that is one of the theories why darkies were born. Utter disaster was only avoided by the prompt action of Jupiter, and Phaethon was turned into a river for his pains. He must have been a most attractive person, and bears a strange resemblance to some of our own younger drivers, but such recklessness is not the general rule, however great applause it may draw from the spectators, who are always the most excited people on the racecourse.

Perhaps it is strange that they should be so, or at least appear outwardly the most moved, while the drivers of the cars themselves rarely show anything but an impassive front. Yet the same sort of relation exists between an actor and his audience, when the former, though in his case he wears a mask of emotion, is really less stirred by his actions than the latter. Day after day he weeps passionately and tears out the hairs of his wig, outward symbols of an agitation far less deep than moves those who behold him, for whom they have all the power of a new or unaccustomed excitement. So it is with the crowds at a motor race. They are swept by wave upon wave of varying moods that often become quite contradictory. At the back of their hearts is a gnawing desire for a fatal accident, and yet, when it comes, they are thoroughly upset. They enter wildly into the enjoyment of thrills which they would hate to provide, and are alternately remarkable for great sportsmanship and entire lack of consideration. When Malcolm Campbell was unlucky in starting, they gave him round upon round of encouraging cheers; yet when his beloved car was burnt out, in a few minutes they had stripped it, under his eyes, of anything they could get for a souvenir. After an accident, they are only too anxious to assist, yet they do their utmost to cause one, by throwing flowers, even cabbages, at their favourite as he passes. Alive to the slightest irregularity on the track, they would probably not notice if somebody in the crowd fainted by their side, and they come in hundreds of thousands to a spectacle about which most of them are quite ignorant. All sizes and sexes pack themselves together as closely as they can, prepared to stand all day and keep awake all night, surely a fine testimony to the finest sport. For such a vast body, the range of moods in its voice is amazing; it seems equally able to cheer decisively, excitedly, adoringly, respectfully, even sadly, and communicate its humours to the drivers. If we provide it with a few hours' contrast to the dullness of everyday life, it is hardly less stirring for us to race between vast intent throngs capable of such abrupt and chimerical changes.

It will not be difficult for these people, who have seen a great race and appreciated its thrills, to picture the events in which I have taken part, however badly I may arrange the canvas, but there are others to whom Brooklands, Le Mans, Dublin, Belfast, are hitherto a closed book, and need some explanation. It is for these that I have written most of the preceding pages, though I should be sorry if they failed in interest for everybody else. I gave my opinion at the start that motor racing was the finest and most thrilling sport in the world to put them in the right mood, and prepare them for later enthusiasm. I devoted some time to praise of the cars, which are really responsible for the excitement, and tried to persuade you that they are not mere bunches of metal, but possess life of their own, waiting for someone to inspire. When you see photographs of the latest models in action – none of which to my mind can convey the full measure of speed – do not forget that beneath those long gleaming lines there is a construction quite as beautiful, and far more subtle, embodying the furthest advances in the science of cars. This I have emphasised because it is too little appreciated, and because I do not wish to exaggerate the prominence of the drivers themselves, when the one most mentioned is myself. But I have not grudged them any of the honour they deserve, nor yet added anything superhuman to their credit and this will make it easier for the ordinary reader to put himself in their place, and live the races he was not privileged to watch. Incidentally it lightens my own task; I shall be at liberty to describe what I saw, and what happened, without turning my recollections into material for a novel.

So summon what motoring experience you have to your aid, and imagine yourself at the wheel of my Bentley. If you have had a crash, recall the sickening at heart as it happened, and if you have travelled fast, think of the wind rushing by and the people turning round and the exhilarated feeling you had. Or if you own a very slow car, remember that marvellous run you had when it touched 45 downhill, double the excitement, let the landscape rush by twice as fast, cling twice as desperately to the steering wheel, picture the awful possibilities of twice as many accidents, and go 90 with me. You are cooped into a tiny cockpit alone, with a strip of windscreen in front of your eyes, in overalls, goggles and a crash helmet, with this great eager machine throbbing beneath you. A corner approaches, the Dundonald hairpin, the Gough Memorial Bend, and you calculate swiftly how soon you must brake and change. The crowds lean over almost touching you, rank upon rank, all shouting, all staring with excited faces, then suddenly quiet; you take the turn, and the noise breaks out again and there is a long even stretch of road shining ahead. Other cars roar behind you, and, according to your policy, you let them pass or press your foot down and leave them fainter and fainter behind; you bear down on little Austins scurrying bravely away from you, eat them up like a ravening dragon and race on. Exaggerate the excitement, if you think it possible, to catch the illusion of being in control yourself; and if there is an accident, picture it while you read about it. See it coming, and feel the resignation of doing your best with little hope of avoiding it. Hear the terrible screeching of the brakes, and the screams of the onlookers; everything seems to be crashing down on top of you, or rising to meet you, as you twist the wheel, and suddenly shoot forward, while the car tears uncontrollably across the track, coming to rest very probably with you underneath it, wondering vaguely if you are killed or going to be burnt. Other cars go roaring past within inches, and then there is a commotion and you are pulled out, very often unhurt. This sentence may imply a callous attitude, but the proportion of serious injuries to the number of ugly-looking accidents is reassuringly small. So the same drivers are enabled year after year to renew their old rivalries and take the same cars round corners full of memories, both pleasant and unpleasant, and the feud makes up in continuity what it lacks in bitterness. If the outsiders do not win, the favourites are sure to make a magnificent race. It is their tradition, and the tradition of their cars.

I have never been able to understand why, with all the vast material lying idle, no one has manufactured an epic out of a motor race; few have so much as drawn from it for simile. Other kinds of speed have had their literary advertisement: Wallace, in *Ben Hur,* did for the chariot what Browning in "How We Brought the Good News from Ghent to Aix" did for the horse; and recently Masefield has immortalised in "Right Royal" the glories of horse-racing proper, and paid a just tribute to an event of which England is proud. But is there not as much, and more, to be proud of in the triumph of British industry that produced the Bentley conquest at Le Mans? Why has nobody woven that wonderful story into a poem, when the cars raced all through the night, and crowds slept in the glare of the headlights, under the trees that line the road? It is a Poet Laureate's duty, and I will drive him round the course at high speed, if it will help him. Perhaps he has difficulty in finding a rhyme for awkward words like "Bentley" and "crankshaft", but such considerations should not hinder some of our younger and more modern poets. Or perhaps aesthetic minds shrink from motor racing, and think it a trifle too vulgar, or a great deal too noisy for their taste. It is none the less lamentable, that the honour of great verse should be withheld from a subject that so merits and suits it, and that the labour and genius involved in a racing car should be without classic praise. Had Shakespeare, who was, I believe, not untainted with vulgarity, lived now, he would have had a word or two to say, and even amended one of his most famous passages to

> "I see you stand like Bentleys in the pits,
> Straining upon the start."

I can waste no more time on this matter, for the end is reached of what I now confess to have been ten pages of deceit. I have disguised under the designation of Chapter One, what was really nothing more than an introduction; but I know quite well, that had I been honest and called it an introduction, nobody would have read it.

— CHAPTER II —

Myself

I SERVED my apprenticeship to racing in 1921 at Brooklands, driving a D.F.P., in those days a fine make, but now forgotten. I had few adventures, but among the few, one as dangerous as any in later years. While travelling at 85 m.p.h., a good speed at the time, I ran a big end bearing; luckily I could draw the car into the side of the track, and, on looking at this trouble, found another far more serious. Both shacklepins, which hold the springs to the frame, were broken and on the point of collapse. Had the lesser accident not occurred first, I should have driven on, ignorant of the greater, at nearly 90 m.p.h. The pins would have collapsed, the front axle probably slip backwards, and nothing could have stopped the car overturning.

I saw, and still see in this, something like the working of Providence, that so caused me to pull up on the verge of disaster. It is on occasions as unforeseen as this, that the driver's skill, however great, and the engine of the car, however efficient, are quite powerless.

I did not race again, for business reasons, until the spring of 1927 when I entered for the Six-Hour Race at Brooklands with my brother Archie. I was a member of the Bentley team, my car being fitted with steel valve rockers, while the other three had them made of duralumin. The other three broke down, and I was overtaking George Duller, who is at home on a horse as he is in a car, when I came in to refill. Kensington Moir, my team manager then and many happy years after, called to me to go right into the pits, and hardly had I obeyed when another driver had been popped into the car and driven off. I was disconcerted, to say the very least of it; however he had gearbox trouble and finished only third. I often think that, had I then my present experience, not a crane would have pulled me out of my seat; but my second thoughts are, that my present experience would have taught me better than to disobey the team manager.

The Six-Hour Race in the following year was the first big event I won, driving a Bentley, in which I completed the greatest distance. It was also remarkable for one of Lord Howe's earliest appearances in the sport, of which he is now a master. Fresh from the courts of Parliament and the police, he was forced to retire after reaching 110 m.p.h., "without," in his own words, "so much as seeing a policeman." Ramponi, the Italian, was also a competitor, driving an Alfa-Romeo. When he turned into the pits to change a wheel, he found for some reason that there was no jack large enough. Furiously he flung jack after jack aside, and finally crawled underneath and turned himself into one, lifting up the whole car as if it was a chair. He was about to restart, when the officials told him that if all the jacks were not put back in the pit, he would be disqualified; but as he knew no English, and they no Italian, babel ensued, followed by an involved interchange of signs, the officials not being able to touch the jacks, nor Ramponi to understand why he should. In the end he flung them all into the pit, regardless of the occupants, who were unused to such treatment, and rushed off storming.

My love of cars, then great, was so increased by my success, that all other ideas vanished, and I resolved to turn motor racing from a hobby into a profession. I had the technical knowledge, but I found great difficulty in getting my father's leave. One of my brothers had been killed in the war, the other in the motor-cycling T.T. Race in the Isle of Man, and he was naturally terrified that I, the last, should meet the same fate. To consent was most gallant, but he could never bear to watch my races, and had them compressed into telegrams sent off every half hour by my secretary, who found it very hard to reach a post office through the crowded course, and, when he did reach it, almost impossible to get inside. But until the bulletin arrived, my father would see nobody, speak to nobody, and take no food;

and the Birkin family provided living examples of perpetual motion, myself tearing round the track, and my father pacing up and down his study.

He must have needed more courage to face the race in the abstract, than I for the actual fact, but I think that, even had he refused consent, he could not have destroyed, nor yet cooled, a passion that so dominated me.

My heart and soul are given up to it. In business that does not interest me, I am hopelessly vague and inefficient, but on a subject in which I am absorbed, just as hopelessly talkative and meticulous. Reporters have come for interviews, expecting to worm the words out of me, and gone away gasping, wondering how late they are for their next appointment. But I have very seldom spoken in public; it bores me as much as my audience, I cannot remember what I was going to say, and when I can, forget how to say it; nor is my confusion aided by a stammer.

If this information disappoints my younger readers, if they had pictured me as tall and broad and clear-cut, barking out instructions in a voice like a knife, I am heartily sorry; I am quite small, and I do stammer.

But once I am in the car, when there is no need to talk or concentrate on anything but the race, all my awkwardness disappears. I feel at home, I feel as happy as a king. But I must know from the outset every single joint, nut, screw and bolt in it, otherwise I am ill at ease. Many very fine drivers rely on perfect preparation by their mechanics, and only touch the machine when they finally get into it, without any knowledge short of the essentials. Very often they win, but for my part, even if certain of invariable defeat, I could not bear to be on terms of such nodding acquaintance with my car.

So, when it is in its cradle, months before the test comes, I wander round, poking it here and prodding it there, probably a confounded nuisance to the whole staff, but acquiring such a familiarity with every detail that any change in the engine's tone is like a voice. It warns me if something is wrong, and, when I demand an extraordinary effort, tells me whether it is equal to it or not. Instead of mere man and machine, we are one mind, though such a relation may make the race harder for me. For I know intimately the strain I put upon each part of the engine, I am aware of the tension and the heat of every tiny screw, while the drivers who are not mechanics can concentrate entirely on speed. They are lapped, as regards the engine, in confident oblivion.

To me inefficiency before the race is as unpardonable as recklessness during it, because with both you are asking something from the car which you have no right to expect; and although luck must play a big part in racing, careful preparation will negative much misfortune.

Accidents must occur, that is the gift of Fate. That they occur continually with the same man, the penalty of ignorance.

But even I, with an unbounded confidence in my machine and happiness in driving it, have never dared to fly in the face of superstition. My brother was killed the day after a dinner-party of thirteen, from which he was the first to rise, and I will have nothing to do with the number. I have refused to go to a dinner-party before a race because it was held on the thirteenth, and am as likely to compete on that date as dash deliberately into a wall. I cling to idiosyncrasies of dress, and should not like to drive without my blue and white scarf, or the crash helmet with my old St. Christopher in it that I have had since 1927. I also wear a sort of glorified tummy band, which is invaluable. It keeps my inside together when I am being jolted up and down for hours on end, and in an accident might prevent the steering wheel from driving into my lungs.

But I do not undergo rigorous training, though a man must be more than usually fit to race. I do not spring out of bed with the dawn and trip round Belfast before breakfast, or restrict myself to a diet of nuts. Though the physical strain of driving a heavy Bentley, well but not marvellously sprung, is great and the strength needed to keep it on the road considerable, it is my mind that is exhausted at the finish.

It is the mechanics, whose bodies are tired, who deserve more than half the praise lavished on the drivers.

They are the real heroes. Months before the public ever hears of the race, they are beginning on the car they mean to win with. It is not a leisurely industry; the very smallest, the almost unnoticeable member is the product of many hours' labour, and even then may have to be removed, re-examined and recommenced. All day they slave and sweat, while the man who is going to drive their work spends his time as he pleases. But as their labour absorbs them, and the construction slowly rises out of a few unconnected parts into its consummation, they begin to feel the affection of the creator. Each man sees the detail for which he was responsible, set ready to perform a task, without which the whole is useless; and as people begin to come and wonder at the finished product, and the first murmurings about the race leak out, and the first paragraphs appear in the press, he feels a jealousy that others should commandeer what he has come to regard as his own. For months he has had it to himself and suddenly all this excitement springs up and he is pushed to one side, and strangers try to take his place.

Resentment gives way to a certain shyness and reticence; he proclaims his certainty of victory, but will give away no secret reasons for it, and as he hears about other competitors and finds them equally assured, he returns feverishly to his own car and refuses to have anything to do with curious inquirers.

As the race draws nearer, and the driver begins to take an interest, pestered with doubts and suggestions and misgivings, his energy beggars description. It carries him on far into the night, bending over the engine, examining, revising, and calculating over and over again the smallest alteration to produce an extra mile. Nothing is too insignificant, no other interest, health or family or rest or sleep, precious enough to deflect his attention.

On the eve of the race, one or more mechanics sleep beside the car, guarding it as a dragon a fairy princess, starting up at every sound. The morning of the race dawns, there is a last frantic inspection, and they stand back, each man represented by some part of the engine or body, and survey their child in silence.

After that it is rudely seized from them by the driver, and they are compelled to watch it passively from the pits, recognising from its tone, even when far away, whether they are to be rewarded or not. There is so little they can do, once it is out of their hands. They are helpless after being indispensable, and have to see their work either driven to death, or paraded in somebody else's triumph. They are given no credit for success, and all the blame for failure. No wonder that I, after receiving gladly the flowers and plaudits of victory, should feel thoroughly ashamed of myself.

It is a little surprising that the Press, which has duly no interest in a race without a stunt, should not have squeezed one out of this, but hitherto praise has been given the driver beyond his merits, and none at all to the tired, unshaven mechanic. I have tried to correct this a little, from indignation and deep personal gratitude. He is far too modest and spellbound by his work to demand any eulogy, and would not know what to do with the orchids and pink carnations. He is only conscious of playing his part in a team, in which the driver has to play his, a shorter one. To race for himself alone is not just foolish, it is nearly impossible, unless he is not a member of a team. He drives for his team, doing what they expect, when he drives well; when he drives for himself, he runs selfishly the risk of breaking his car in competition with his team mates.

Yet he too has moments as nerve-racking as the mechanic. Most bachelor drivers agree with me, finding more unpleasantness in the hour before the start than in the rest of their lives. The three days previous have been spent in practice, when I am torn between a desire to go as fast as possible, and the haunting dread of ruining the car before the race. I have never been able to get this idea out of my head, whether it is based on a real or an imagined alarm. I have no thought of injury to myself, because all my attention and anxiety and hope are concerned not with myself, but with my car. The small part of the crowd with a genuine interest in technical difficulties and a closer intelligence of the point of motor racing, watch me practising with critical and unbiassed eyes. I have to fight the frowns of the mechanics and not be too elated by their smiles. Finally, with all my tremblings for my own machine and admiration of other people's, I have to acquire such a perfect knowledge of the circuit itself, that every irregularity in its surface is awaited and provided for, every bend and bump learnt by heart, and my own course so mapped out, definite and invariable, that I continually cover my own tracks.

The first practice, especially on a new circuit, should be taken with caution. The existence of danger does not mean a red flag, and so I found to my cost on the Boulogne course in 1928.

At one point there is a steep hill, with a hump back, and, once over this, a long straight stretch ahead. I was going extremely fast on my first practice, driving in the middle and seeing nothing to hinder a clear run. I reached the hump back, and suddenly the car was flung right across to the extreme left of the road, with the left hand wheel in the hedge. Had it skidded six inches further, the car would have overturned without a doubt, and serious injury only been avoided by other hands than mine. I finished the course, and started off again. This time I treated the hump back with respect, clinging to the right hand side of the road. Again the car was flung over to the left, but only so far as the middle. I could continue unperturbed, at every fresh practice taking the hill faster until I knew it so well that I hardly thought about it.

There is the same danger for novices on the Belfast road. At one stage it bends gradually to the right, not sufficiently to check the speed of those that know it well. But there is a curious little bump breaking a surface otherwise level, and many have been the punishments of not finding it. The car is thrown so far to the left as you go over it that you cannot approach it in the middle of the road without being flung straight over to the left bank at high speed; and even when you take it on the extreme right, as near the inside of the curve as possible, you must have all your wits about you to keep the car on the road and continue on round the right-hand bend. It is here that precious seconds are lost or gained, drivers who know the policy with mechanical accuracy being able to travel at 120 m.p.h., when the less acquainted have no choice but to slow down.

But neither the most penetrating knowledge of the course, the most successful practice runs, nor the highest opinion of my car, have ever reconciled me with that last hour or two before the start. Every second as it approaches steals away my faith and my courage, until, drained of them both, I am left with another hundred minutes to wait.

A devilish steward, who can never have raced himself, ordained that the cars should be in line at least an hour before the flag went down. There are two orders in which they may be arranged in real Grand Prix, for racing cars and not standard models "hotted up," in Swedish drill line with rows of three each, in alternate spacing behind each other. In this event, a back place is a misfortune hard to overcome until the front ranks have spread out and may leave you in the lurch at the first corner. In other races, the cars are drawn up next to each other, their tails to the side of the track, their bonnets pointing into the middle. The order is sometimes decided by last year's result, or the big cars may be put in front, the smaller having a certain number of laps for handicap, and when the flag falls, the drivers sprint across the track, leap in and start the terrible jostling for position.

But long before this, everything is ready, and I have little to do but wait. Then I am seized with utter misery and blank despair. All around the crowds are laughing, peering at the cars, and making it quite obvious that they at least are not excited. The mechanics are quite calm; the team manager is quite calm, making sure that his instructions are finally understood. Only I am in a turmoil, and, looking down the line, see the other drivers in the same state, sitting apart and talking nervously to no one in particular. Time after time I go across to the car, put it out of gear, put it in again, make sure that the starting switch is in order. The crowds surge round and ask intelligent questions but my answers are generally so rude and abrupt that they ask no more, and go away with the impression that I am a thoroughly disagreeable old man.

My friends come up and offer their good wishes, which I accept with a wan smile. All the time I tell myself that I shall get a bad start and be left at the corner, that the car will not start at all and be left completely, and then I go across and fiddle with the gears and switch again. Strangers bring their autograph albums to be signed; it is a welcome distraction, and I sign them all. Small boys fix me with a grim stare, and when I glare to make them go away, smile reassuringly and continue to stare. For a little while everyone turns round, as the celebrity of the day arrives, and bands play the National Anthem; then they turn back to the cars. The only relief is from cigarettes, which I smoke in dozens and throw away before they are finished. I walk up and down while someone babbles of religion, art, politics and other things of no importance, to take my mind off the subject of the race. Everyone is very kind and interested, but it would be more helpful if they were damnably rude or actively aggressive.

Slowly the crowds begin to turn off the track, and the cars are left forlorn, gaping at us. This is the worst moment of all, when I wait for the starter to drop his flag. I can do nothing more for the engine before the race begins. Have I left it in gear, or have I put it out? I am so convinced of both that I can be certain of neither.

And then the flag falls, I tear across, leap in, and of course get away without the slightest trouble.

Immediately all my despair and anxiety drop, like a cloak off my shoulders; ever to have entertained them seems silly, when the car darts forward so eagerly and the crowd raises its first cheers.

At first I am pushing through the jumble to try and reach my position for the corner, but once round, the car draws away from the many slower, and settles down to the early laps. The thrill of speed quickens in me, but it is an old and expected thrill; to it are added the newer triumph of passing other cars, and the joy of losing my nervousness. I take the course upon which I have spent the last days' practice, but this is the race, this is the climax, there is nothing to stop me, nothing in front to dread. I have a mania for the gearbox and as I feel the car slip without noise, save the bang of the exhaust, from top to third, from third to second, then up again into top and away instantly at over 100, I become a part of the machine. I begin to thrill to the harmony of driver growing more mechanical and car more human, without which the full glory of the race is unattainable. I have no fears for myself; if danger threatens, I feel no shock or sinking at heart, only confidence that the car will pull me through. In return for the life I gave it at the start, it now inspires me, and we fly round as one. To know this is all that matters; if anything is amiss, the engine will warn me, and, bitter though my disappointment, I am at least prepared for it. As a rider of his mount, I am in control, but of something far more powerful and divine, with which it is impossible to be frightened. I was much more afraid when a car in which I was once being driven in London, crashed into a 'bus, or on board the airplane Hannibal, when the propellers broke in mid-air.

Soon, too, I begin, as it were, to absorb the surroundings, remember here a clump of trees, there a coloured hoarding. At one corner there will be some of my backers cheering, at the next a man with glasses leaning over the rails. I pass casualties, wildly trying to push their wreck on to the road, and if it is a long distance race, I hand over to my fellow-driver. The idea angers me so, that I almost race by the pits and leave him, but the foulest of all crimes is disobedience to the pit manager and the car drives away without me, leaving a passion to be off once more myself, to restore all my old nervousness. Weary though I am, I cannot sleep because of the talking in the pits and the familiar voice of the car every few minutes. I can never believe someone else is driving it as well as I, though he is driving it far better, and I am ready to take over long before the time.

The race goes on, and the excitement of the crowd swells, and the numbers of the cars sweep up on to the scoreboard. More drop out, more wrecks lie at the roadside. Then perhaps that awful hour comes, when a new note in the engine warns me of trouble, and before I can reach the pits, I have joined the wrecks.

The cars I have driven have been so carefully prepared by the mechanics that this has only happened to me on a few occasions. But they were dismal indeed. I jumped out, trying to be calm, and, when I found it hopeless to go on, walked back in misery to watch the others finish.

But those rare moments, when I have won, have been far and away the most glorious of my career and the feeling of them the most wonderful. Sometime before the end I was aware of victory, and at the beginning of my last lap the crowd began to cheer. All the way the noise increased, and as I came round the final bend into the straight, I could see the people rising to their feet in the stands and pushing to the sides of the track. Hats were waved and the applause here was louder than ever; as I drew up, I found I was shaking from excitement. But when I was about to step out, an indescribable whirlpool seemed to catch hold of me, lift me from my seat, smother me with flowers, hang them round my neck, force them into my hands and pour glassfuls of champagne down my throat. All my concentration deserted me shamefully, and I was dazed, vague and happy beyond all words. The team of which I was part forced their way through, to give me the praise they themselves deserved. Friends thumped me on the back, and people who seemed complete strangers crowded round to congratulate me. I could see nothing but heads, smell nothing but flowers, hear nothing but cheering. Everyone was enjoying my good fortune as much as I, some laughing, some crying, and the foreigners kissing. Whenever there was a lull, and only a hundred people shouting instead of a thousand, several bands struck up the National Anthem in their favourite keys, as a signal for redoubled cheers. While all the time, the real hero of the race, the person for whom this was the crown of months of preparation, more, the purpose of a lifetime, the low, dusty, almost unobserved car, stood quiet and contented as people scrambled all over it, cooling itself after its exertion, panting a little because it was tired, with a wreath of flowers draped across its bonnet.

Not for a long while was the excitement over. There was a prize-giving and no race to watch. The people would have no more of this for some time; they were out for their money's worth. It was a good hour before I got away myself, forcing a path through the press with the car's mudguards. So I reached my hotel and there I thought of the following day, of talking over each lap with the team and my friends, of receiving telegrams and hearing the stories of other drivers. I thought of the days long before, when the car was only a few screws and strips of steel, and our calculations not yet reinforced by hope, of the perseverance of the mechanics and my own apprehension, and at last, with the sound of the traffic still sorting itself out in the streets and such memories jumbling in my mind, I got into bed and, not unaided by champagne, fell fast asleep.

— CHAPTER III —

A Race

My next was my first big race on the Continent, and one of the finest events in the racing year. It takes place at Le Mans, the famous French road course, and is naturally an entirely different affair from anything at Brooklands. This I add, in case anyone should imagine an ordinary road course to be provided with elaborate banking, and traversed at a speed never less than 100 miles an hour.

The lap is 10.7 miles long, and the race is over a period of 24 hours, starting at 4 p.m. on Saturday and ending, for those that do end, at 4 p.m. on Sunday; in 1928 the dates were June 17th and 18th. The reward of victory is the Rudge-Whitworth Cups. A certain distance, or number of laps, has to be covered by each car, varying with the capacity of the different engines, and the car exceeding this distance by the most miles, at the end of the 24 hours, wins. There is also a prize for each class, from the highest cubic capacities, that is, the cars with most litres, to the lowest, and another for the greatest number of laps covered by any car at all.

It is a wonderful test of endurance and speed and efficiency, and perhaps profits the different firms and nations more than any other event. The cars are standard models, and, but for a few alterations permitted in the rules, could be bought by any one on the ordinary market, and their success or failure at Le Mans has a large influence upon their popularity. They race all night and their headlights have to last from sunset to sunrise, while the car travels at 100 m.p.h. on many stretches, and averages at least 65. It has been said that to finish satisfactorily at Le Mans is a guarantee of 20,000 miles on high roads for 6 years to an owner who does not give the engine any harsh treatment. Each car is allowed two drivers, in case of accident and they must carry what spare parts they need with them, none being permitted in the pits except an extra wheel.

The course is shaped like a wishbone, with Le Mans and Pontlieue corner at the joint. One prong is about 5 miles long, a straight road to Mulsanne and the White House, where the disaster of 1927 was staged; the other is as straight but shorter, about 3 miles, as far as Arnage, where there is an equally abrupt turn. The two extremes of Arnage and Mulsanne are joined by a two and a half mile strip of road; it is straight after the hairpin at Mulsanne for over a mile, and then swerves into a twist toward the inside of the course, which makes, with the hairpin at Arnage, the famous S-bend. To have called Arnage and Mulsanne corners hairpins, is an exaggeration, but they cannot be taken at much over 30 miles an hour.

The whole of this part of the road runs between thick set trees, under which the most enthusiastic spectators pitch their tents for the night. The rest of the course lies amongst heather, which is usually invisible for the crowds. For days before the race, the road is covered with workmen setting up and strengthening palings. The pits and grandstands face each other half-way down the shorter prong of the wishbone. Every year they have spread like a bungaloid growth, and in that year they covered at least 300 yards. Diplomatic Frenchmen hang them lavishly with the flags of all nations, until, with their fronts like shop windows and the counters with mechanics behind them, they give a good imitation of a high street in Shopping Week. In front and on top of them and of the grandstand, wherever there is any room not required for spectators, you are confronted by titanic hoardings in the brightest colours, advertising cars, petrols, oils, spare parts, and insurance policies. To an advertisement agent there can be nowhere more like Paradise, and he lets his imagination run riot.

The preparations before the race are as those of a Rabelaisian banquet. Special trains, special boats, special aeroplanes, are run at special fares. Journalists have every possible machine put at their disposal to get them back with their reports and photographs for the evening editions. Most newspapers are represented, and the bustle of the more specialised is terrific. In the pit of one of them, English tea was served on both afternoons by French waiters, and a frieze installed with witty caricatures of the competitors. The sight of the crowds pushing their way towards the cars, hiding them completely from view, of the tents pitched ready for the night, of the picnics and the programme sellers, with the broad racecourse threading its ways through the midst, is like the outlook over Epsom Downs on Derby Day.

The narrow streets of Le Mans, an important town which falls asleep again as soon after the race as possible, are full of traffic. Battalions of gendarmes blow their whistles, and regiments of foreigners pester them for information. Several drivers in the race were nearly imprisoned for continually disregarding a "One Way Street" notice they could not understand, and blocking all passage for half a morning. Even the inhabitants, few of whom are in the habit of ever leaving Le Mans, grow aware that a contest of some sort is to be held, and develop a frantic excitement. They learn from their country's press that they are shortly to behold, not a circus, but "Une manifestation interessante en tous regards, utilite, sport et spectacle emouvante." The utility interests them, the sport has their admiration, and the spectacle emouvante drives them almost to hysteria. Their hospitality, and that of all the French motor clubs, is magnificent, and there is a great deal of fraternising.

Such was the scene upon which I came, thrilled and rather frightened by the prospect of so great an event. I was one of the Bentley team, driving number 3 with the veteran Chassagne, a name always simplified into "Chass." He was acknowledged to be one of the finest drivers in France, with an experience as wide as any in Europe. He had not raced in England since he went over the top at Brooklands in 1922, when, like most people who are thrown out of their cars, on that occasion he left his shoes behind him. Usually his attire is a model of neatness; he wears white kid gloves, and nothing can perturb him. At that time he must have been forty-seven, but as energetic in doing his job as any younger, and more efficient. He never made a fuss, but if any expected or unexpected assistance could be given, he gave it. In England he would long ago have been a martyr to the craze for Grand Old Men, but in his own country he was not troubled, his modesty was an example to all, and he treated fledgling drivers as his equals. His performance in this race I have always claimed as its most remarkable feature.

The other two Bentleys were driven, number 2 by Clement and Dr Benjafield, and old number 4, the first in last year's terrible crash, by Rubin and Babe Barnato. They were most anxious to maintain the car's record of recent triumphs; both the 1924 and 1927 Le Mans had gone to a Bentley, and also the Grand Prix at Montlhéry in 1925 and 1927. But a keener edge was put on their anxiety by the competition of the American Black Hawk Stutz, and a team of Chryslers. For some time the interest of the motoring world had been focussed on Indianapolis, the American track, where a great struggle between Stutz and Hispano had recently been fought. It was hoped that an English car might enter the list against one at least of these giants, and now the time had come.

The Chryslers were reputed to have increased their powers of endurance. They had only three speeds, the ratio between top and second gear being so high that nothing lower would be necessary.

Much too had been heard of an Itala, a French make, to be driven by the great Benoist and d'Auvergne. It had been practising for some time in Paris, up and down the spiral ramp of a famous garage, between the first and second floor, and there was a variety of very fast and efficient smaller cars.

All three Bentleys were painted a vivid green, which was Britannia's official racing colours. The Stutz was a saturnine black, and the Chryslers, or one of them at least, pure white. It could not have been hard for the spectators to distinguish these three from the throng of blues and greys and reds, and recognise them when still a long way off.

So the normal importance of this race was emphasised by national competition, the innovations and the experiments, and the Pride of the Bentleys; and I felt I was indeed lucky to be at the wheel of my 4½-litre, unsupercharged number three. My nervousness before the start was proportionately great, but at last we were off, down the straight towards Pontlieue, with the three Bentleys almost arm in arm at the head of a long procession. When I came round just in front of Babe Barnato on the first lap, I found Baron d'Erlanger had only then left the post in his Lagonda. He seemed not the least flustered, and all through a race which was to have plenty of thrills for him, he thoroughly justified his nickname of *Poker Face* and his reputation for courageous driving. Behind me was Clement in the other Bentley, and, unpleasantly close, the murmuring of the Black Hawk. We knew that it was not so fast as our Bentleys, that, if pressed, we could outdistance it for some time, but we did not want to be forced into this extra speed and run the risk of imperilling our engines. Further behind were the Chryslers and a Lagonda and already Laly in his Aries had fallen out, owing to trouble with a big end bearing. As far as I could see, the 1500 c.c. Salmson was setting the pace for the smaller cars. For that first lap I averaged 72.7 miles an hour, a record at once beaten by Barnato with 74.19, and then again by me with 74.9. But the Bentley supremacy was shortlived as far as records were concerned. The Black Hawk, which persisted in clinging on to our tails and setting a tremendous pace, averaged 75.4.

It was plain from the start, then, that the race was going to be won at a very great speed, and that most of last year's records, but for accidents, would be beaten long before the finish. The thought gave me the greatest pleasure, especially as the car was running perfectly, I was leading, and felt perfectly in tune with the engine.

We were not quite sure whether the Stutz was content to lie behind us, or wanted to pass and could not, or whether we were hindering it, but after a protest from its driver, Brisson, Barnato was warned that he was too far on the left-hand side of the road, and might have hampered the Stutz. But Brisson himself, in the most sportsmanlike way, deliberately went round to the Bentley pits after changing over, and declared that, in actual fact, he had not been hampered at all. His fellow-driver was called Bloch, whose excitement was so great when he was filling up, that he emptied cans of petrol into the tank long after it was full, and there were pools all over the ground.

On the sixth lap the Stutz fell behind a little, and I drew a breath of relief; but on the seventh lap, a brief shower of rain fell, and as I wiped the water off my goggles, I found that it had come up again, and on the eleventh lap it actually averaged 76.01 miles per hour and broke its own record. It was going alarmingly fast, and running very smoothly, but after this effort it dropped back a little, and Babe Barnato a lap or two later got round at 76.16.

It was a glorious race; on almost every lap the record had been broken. I was still leading, with Babe close behind me, and the Black Hawk menace not quite so prominent. But the first hour with a string of twenty-three more to come, was hardly the time for confidence and I felt most happy to realise what a struggle there was going to be.

During the next few laps an accident occurred, which very nearly turned into something as serious as the disaster the previous year. It was at the identical place on the Mulsanne bend, and was caused by Samuelson in his Lagonda. His driving, and his cornering particularly, had been extremely wild, and whenever I was near him, I kept my eyes well skinned. His pit signalled to him many times to slow down, but evidently he did not see the signals, while d'Erlanger, in the other Lagonda, was obeying his instructions to go faster and catch up the time he had lost at the start. D'Erlanger approached Mulsanne at high speed, and had just rounded the corner, when he saw Samuelson's Lagonda sliding down a sandbank into the middle of the track. There was no chance of avoiding it; he braked as much as he could and ran straight into the back. Clive Gallop, in the third Lagonda, was 400 yards behind He saw the crowds running in the direction of the corner, shouting and pointing, and with great presence of mind, just slowed down enough to avoid joining the wreckage.

Samuelson's car was not as damaged as d'Erlanger's, but the crash had pushed it so far into the bank, that he could not get it on to the road again. He began to dig frantically with his hands to disengage the wheels. But he made little headway, and at last one of the spectators ran to a neighbouring farm, borrowed a spade, and threw it noisily in Samuelson's way. In decent time, Samuelson noticed it, and, after two hours' valiant digging, got the car out, but found it impossible to continue. D'Erlanger's car, however, could continue at once, and was taken into the pits. There the unruffled baron, who was badly cut about the nose and cheeks, handed over to Douglas Hawkes, who examined the car, and finally drove it off with no front wheel brakes or shock absorbers. He frequently averaged 65 mph., and completed the whole twenty-four hour course, by a fine exhibition of skill and control.

About the twentieth lap I was still in front, approaching the top of the hill after Pontlieue at about 105 mph. It is my practice here to change into third at 80, using the change to help brake the car, change down once more at 50, and go round the corner at about 30. The Bentley was running beautifully; I had every hope of retaining my lead. All sorts of pleasant things might have happened if a horse shoe nail had not run into the back tyre, which at once went flat, while the car skidded into the grass at the side.

I was then slowing down, but none the less travelling at 100 mph; and so, for 40 or 50 yards before I could pull up, the tyre disintegrated, all the canvas jammed between the wheel and the brake drum and the right-hand back wheel was hopelessly locked. I jumped out, trying to persuade myself that everything would be all right, to find an appalling tangle that looked as if nothing could unravel it.

But it was no good to waste time lamenting and cursing. I must have a jack at once.

Now, a short while before the race, it was decided that the Bentleys should all carry as little weight as possible and, as it would be easy to go 50 or 60 at least, so we were told, on a flat tyre and as it was foolish to wait to put on a new wheel, when we would have to stop at all events at the pits with the old, a jack was considered unnecessary and there was not one on the car.

So there I was, six miles from the pits, one wheel immovable, and without the only implement of which I was really in need. My misery was not lightened by the other cars as they swooped past me, nor by the crowds, which clustered round and offered their assistance. To accept it would have meant disqualification, so I was ceaselessly jumping up from the wheel to prevent some well-meant kindness which only increased my difficulties.

There were in my pockets a jack-knife, a file, a hammer and some pliers. With these, for an hour and a half, I hacked at the mass of red-hot material, the molten rubber and the tread that had collected round the wheel. Lap after lap the cars raced round within a few feet of me; the fight between Stutz and Bentley went on without me, and I realised that if anything happened to Babe, the American could not fail to win, for the third Bentley was some way behind and having trouble. If I had not been alone, if I had possessed some powerful, useful tool, I might have entered into the running again. But I had nothing, and was so exhausted that I could scarcely see. I loosened the wheel as much as I dared on the hub, and by rocking the car to and fro, at last managed to loosen the knot.

The tyre was free. I flung it into the car, jumped in sweating and worn out, and began to drive on the rim. It made a hideous noise, and every limb in my body was shaken. But I managed to do 60 mph. with what seemed safety, and thought myself lucky to be in the race once more. Just the sort of thing that would happen - but directly I reached the pits, I would change the wheel, Chassagne would take over, and by furious driving we might possibly pick up much, if not all, of our lost position.

And then, when I had reached Arnage, still three miles from the pits, the rim collapsed. I had been driving it along the grass at the side to save it as much as possible, and when it broke, the back of the car slipped, and the whole machine slid gracefully into the ditch.

I was too wretched then to do anything but run as fast as I could to the pits for the jack that now alone could save utter catastrophe. When I arrived, with all my joints aching and my mind raging, I found there an atmosphere of even deeper gloom.

Immediately I had not appeared in due time, anxiety was felt; when I did not appear five minutes after it, plain horror. The timekeepers sat, like the mother of Sisera, murmuring in distraction, "Why are the wheels of his chariot so long in coming? Why tarry the wheels of his chariot?" until at last the news came of my puncture, and, looking round, they saw all the jacks lying on the counter. They then spent hours waiting for me, in such a state of nerves that no one dared nor yet wanted to utter a word.

When finally I tumbled in exhausted, there was only one man with all his wits about him. Observing quietly, "Maintenant, c'est a moi," old Chassagne picked up a couple of jacks in his arms and started off at a run. He was, I have said, 47 years of age; he ran the whole way; he jacked up the car; he changed the wheel; and when he came into the pits to put on a new spare, the whole crowd rose and cheered him to the echo. He was, however, quite unperturbed.

It was eight o'clock when he started again. We had lost three hours. From being first, we were now miles behind the last, and we had not only not the remotest chance of winning, but very little of completing the distance to qualify for next year. It was the cruellest trick of Fate to choose the one year jacks were not carried. As Chassagne drove on like a man possessed, I heard people stating frankly that it was absurd, that it was hard luck, but we were out of next year's race as much as out of this; and I determined I would prove them wrong.

The duel between Stutz and Bentley was as bitter as ever, now. One leading and now the other and the crowd cheering its favourite wildly as he passed.

Evening had fallen, and night was approaching. At half-past nine, all the cars lit their headlamps, and round the course lights began to leap out of the darkness. In the grandstand they hung in row upon row, shining on the huddled forms of the sleepers, and the pits were like the illumined shop windows of a long street. Across the track in front lay a strip of light. Slowly the headlamps of a car rose above the distant trees, sweeping round a corner and shining among the top branches, as they turned into the straight. They approached, and the humming of the engines rose to a roar, and the glare grew blinding. In the restaurants and dancing hall the music stopped, and the people ran to the side of the track, while the sleepers started to their feet, and then the car plunged for a few seconds out of the dark, like a shadow, into the light, gleamed like silver, and vanished once more, fainter and fainter, with the glow of its two red rear lights pointing its direction.

The Bentleys had a centre lamp of great power and reach, and when it shone in the woods by Mulsanne, the trees stood up like ghosts, and the tents were like white figures with shapes in strange attitudes sprawling round them. There were a few still watching here, but it was very silent and most who were awake preferred to keep awake by dancing. A line of lights beyond Pontlieue showed Le Mans, and the stream of cars always going from and returning to the race.

A little after midnight Rubin took over the Bentley from Babe Barnato. The Stutz was in the pits at exactly the same moment for refuelling and got away first. But when they next came round, Rubin was only 30 yards behind, then 100 yards in front to wild applause, and then a quarter of a mile. But I did not feel jealous of them; I had my own excitement, though the majority had given up my chances of qualifying as hopeless. I was not even considered but the cheers for Babe and Rubin spurred me on, and I drove like an accurate madman.

Dawn brought sunshine over most of the course, but at the evil old Mulsanne Corner an impenetrable cloud of fog had gathered. It was invisible almost until I was enveloped in it, and travelling at 120 mph into the dip, suddenly found I had only the treetops to guide me. Luckily it was not long in clearing, and, though gusts of rain swept the road, the weather was not bad. So Sunday came, and number 2 Bentley found one of its waterpipes was cracked. As refilling was only allowed every 20 laps, it had to give up. I passed Clement and Benjafield wheeling it disconsolately to the mortuary, or dead-car park. At Mulsanne a Salmson had stopped, but another was going very well and actually led on the curve formula of speed. There was no abating the great battle between Stutz and Bentley. At about midday Babe gained 15 seconds on one lap and 50 on the next, finally passing the Americans in the pits to the cheers of a refreshed and excited crowd. I knew I was going well myself and at 2.30, with the sun shining, I passed the pits and saw the Stutz, drawn up, broken, out of the race. Then I realised that Babe was as good as the winner, and felt inspired to follow his example. People had begun to work out my distance, and spread the news that I was going to have a close race. Signals were put out, and as I started on the last lap of all, I knew I had to beat the lap record to qualify. It was announced on the loud-speakers; for the last time I took Mulsanne.

I felt the car go as never before, heard the cheers echoing for Babe's victory, and roared past the stand for good and all. Somebody seemed to be telling me that I had averaged 79, and if I had, I had qualified.

I learnt how the whole pit had given me up and would not believe it could be done, until my mechanic, Chevrollier, heard the voice of the engine, still a long way off, and began to dance up and down shouting, "He's done it!"

It was a pleasant little triumph to poke in after Babe's magnificent victory. He had driven beautifully the whole way, and held his own from the Stutz for over 20 hours. The crowd gave him the great ovation he more than deserved, as they were destined to do yet twice more, after which he decided to close a brilliant racing career.

All seemed satisfied; the Salmsons did splendidly and the Alvises did splendidly. The English entries which failed were delighted that their country had won and the French were happy that their party had been a success. After being frantic with disappointment, I was blissfully content, and altogether, in the words of an eloquent reporter, it was "Un très beau match."

4.5 litre Bentley under construction in the Welwyn workshop. The 16 valve engine was fitted with an Amherst Villiers Roots supercharger producing 182 bhp @ 3,900 rpm - Courtesy Brooklands Museum

Taking the Bentley through its paces at Brooklands - Courtesy Brooklands Motor Museum

A photo taken of Birkin and the Bentley team at The Irish GP - The Geoffrey Goddard Collection

Birkin examining his car's carburettor assembly - Courtesy Brooklands Motor Museum

Preparing the "Blower" Bentley for a Brooklands record attempt - Courtesy Brooklands Motor Museum

Birkin and Jean Chassagne's Bentley passes the 2 Litre Lagonda of Francis Samuelson and F King, which had crashed on lap 14 - Heritage Image Partnership/Alamy Stock Photo

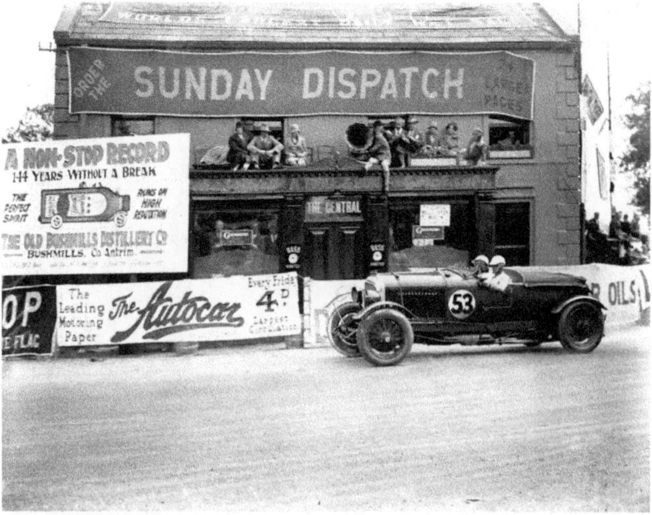

1928 TT. Birkin in his Bentley - The Geoffrey Goddard Collection

Birkin, Clement, Barnato, Benjafield, Rubin and Cook at Brooklands in May 1928 - The Geoffrey Goddard Collection

Bentley 4½ litre in 1928 Coupe Boillot Boulogne -
National Motor Museum, Beaulieu

Frank Clement, Tim Birkin, Wolf Barnato at Le Mans in 1928 -
The Geoffrey Goddard Collection

— CHAPTER IV —

Some Foreigners

Le Mans was followed by the German race on the Nürburg Ring, which I consider one of the finest road courses in the world. Situated in that mountainous district north of the Moselle, just before it joins the Rhine at Coblenz, its myriad curves, dips and heights command a magnificent and diverse view, over woods and valleys stretching for miles, with only a few villages in their folds and houses upon their slopes. Its shape is roughly that of two ovals, joined by a strip upon which pits and grandstands are built; it is over 18 miles long, and the greatest stretch of straight is not more than a mile and a quarter. Every imaginable obstacle known to motor racing is represented: there are 170 curves and hairpin bends, up gradients of 17 to 27 in 100, and down gradients of 11. The race takes a course devised with the greatest ingenuity. The cars leave the start on the smaller oval, four and a half miles in circumference, the end of which brings them back behind the pits on to the larger, of about fourteen miles, with the finish once more in front of the pits. So it is possible to see them at several periods during each lap, and even, with glasses, when they go out upon the hills.

There are really three courses turned into one, and for a 4½-litre Bentley, on every eighteen miles, there are thirty-seven gear changes. Nürburg offers as high a test of a car as any other road on which racing has ever taken place, except the Targa Florio in Sicily, which is rendered more difficult by the poor state of the surface. The Nurburg surface is perfect, made of macadam, nine metres broad, and with very little banking. At one point it rises to a height of two thousand feet, beneath which lie the woody valleys. Far away the Moselle and Rhine wind towards Coblenz, and vineyards slope upwards from their banks.

It is an absolute switchback, the abruptness of the corners, their frequency and the undulation of the road being quite without parallel. It is significant that it should have been built in the two troubled years between 1925 and 1927 to relieve unemployment. It cost over a million pounds, which were defrayed by the City of Cologne, the German Government, and local corporations. No ordinary traffic is allowed on it at any period; it is kept solely for experiment and competition, although one can drive round it for a small payment. In 1928 it had not, of course, begun to pay its way, nor acquired the international reputation it now has, and continues to increase. But it cannot fail to end by working at a profit, since the arrangements for the crowds are as suitable to their taste as the course is to the drivers.

It benefits from having been erected with the one idea of being a racing road course, so while the grandstands give a view commanding most of the race, there are an abundance of beer gardens and teahouses, and conglomeration is avoided by careful Teutonic railing-off. The pits are the very abode of luxury that befits the noble breeds of German cars; they are made of ferro-concrete, and their roofs are not improvised, as elsewhere. An immense scoreboard informs spectators of the state of the race with the greatest speed possible and perfect efficiency, and a loudspeaker brays the number of the approaching cars while they are still a mile and a half away. Many foreigners go to Germany to see an entirely different, perhaps more famous kind of Ring but Bayreuth cannot boast an audience as large as Nürburg. The biggest races are certain to draw a crowd of three-quarters of a million, of whom the majority are Germans from all corners of their country,

They arrive by every manner of transport. Some start several weeks previously, in a pair of khaki shorts and a cricket shirt, and walk the whole way. Large parties may be seen a few days before on bicycles, heading for the mountains, father in front and family grouped behind. A few come by car at the last moment, but mostly foreigners; and on the morning of the race the woods and slopes are covered with migrating hordes.

Each little company has, long before, staked its claim, accurately calculating from which point it will derive most profit. They have no desire for thrills. They do not scream at a skid, or clutch each other in an accident. But they sit by the roadside, in their little hats and open collars, with a notebook in one hand, a pencil in the other, and an assortment of stopwatches on the ground. As the cars come round, they peer at the engines and jot down a short note about each machine, while their wives regulate the stopwatches. Every now and then they take a huge gulp of the beer that is always by their side, and an immense bite of sausage, and begin a serious technical discussion with their neighbours. They know long before the end who will win, as long as there is no disaster, but this does not in the least diminish their ardour; theirs is the attention of a cool critic, not of an onlooker at gladiatorial shows.

To talk to such people is always a rare delight for me, accustomed to the more quixotic moods of the Le Mans and Ulster crowds, and the exciting, but often overpowering hysteria of those farther south. I love sitting with German mechanics, German citizens, and even their wives, whose intimacy with technical niceties is almost as marked, and discussing cars over vast flagons of that wonderful beer. Their hospitality is most generous, and to English challengers, lavish in the extreme. They are fine company, good winners and sporting losers.

Their leading driver is Rudi Carraciola, whose name will be coupled with victory more than once in the following pages. He must be now about thirty, though his list of successes is that of a far older man. Relying entirely on his mechanics for the preparation of his car, and knowing little of its inside himself, he is usually asleep two hours before the flag is due to fall, and arrives on the track a little before the start. He combines colossal speed with the most acute judgment, and I can recall no time at which he has been guilty of recklessness or inaccuracy. The pace he set in his T.T. race in 1929 was one of my most amazing recollections. In the midst of heavy downpours, which hid his white Mercedes in a cloud of spray, he drove continually at 120 m.p.h. and more, holding the heavy car with its left-hand drive, and not appearing for one moment ill at ease. He is very brave, and one of the few men not subject to an attack of nerves before the race begins. His triumphs for the Mercedes Company until 1930 have only been equalled by his own for Alfa-Romeo from then until 1932. His wife plays a conspicuous part in her husband's races, and is a familiar figure in the pits during the event, where she presides over her own team of stopwatches. On one occasion, when women were forbidden in the pits, Frau Carraciola was detected, disguised in overalls, lurking in a dark corner.

I was the only Englishman competing at Nürburg that year, and had no previous experience of the course. On one of my practice runs I took my secretary, Lambert, with me, who has a great affection for the sport, but has not driven so much as a Morris Oxford for the last eight years. We were going down a steep hill at a considerable speed, with a right-angle bend leading straight up a hill from the bottom. There was the usual precipice on one side, and, as I cornered, Lambert was thrown over on to the steering wheel and knocked it out of my hand. The car rocked, but I just managed to catch the wheel in time and right it.

I happened to be the first Englishman to drive a car at Nürburg since the war and I had a most sporting reception when I finished eighth, after a splendid race.

I have never yet had the great pleasure of racing in Italy; but I know something of Italian tracks, and the people who go to them. And, oh! The contrast to the Germans! The latter calm and undramatical; the former shouting, crying, kissing, laughing and cheering as each car thunders by, leaping up in their seats and waving their neighbours' hats. As their favourites go past, "Avanti!" they yell, "Avanti! Coraggio!" and if he is driving without skill, they groan without restraint. There is always something to excite them even if they have to be content with mere speed. There is a crash, and the noise that breaks out must be one of the loudest in the world. Everyone has advice to offer; the crowds press forward to give assistance; enemies triumph, and friends weep.

But under this hysteria there is a profound and genuine enthusiasm for the sport. Signor Mussolini gives it active encouragement, and the drivers are presented to him after the race. He has made motor racing far more popular in Italy than horse racing, almost indeed substituted it. The public do not have to go to specialising newspapers for their information about races and technical improvements. The popular press segregates several columns for the subject, which hints at a popularity not enjoyed so largely in other countries. Every weekend from April to September there is a meeting on one or other of their courses.

So the Italians learn from association what the Germans find out for themselves but they have also a race which for diversity and adventures will stand comparison with Nürburg or any other.

It consists of one enormous lap of a thousand miles, and is run along the high road, which remains open to ordinary traffic. It passes right through the middle of some of the biggest towns, Brescia its headquarters, and among the others Parma, Bologna, Florence, Perugia, Rome, Padua and Verona. There is every possibility of an innocent English tourist family in their Morris meeting a wild stream of roadsters travelling at at least 70 m.p.h., rushing past a picture gallery. The event is attended with terrific excitement. Flags line the whole route, restaurants stay open all night, and a chocolate factory, which is passed on the way, presents each competitor with a large box of candies. Anybody is allowed to help, but so many hundreds of mechanics are posted every few miles, that the crowd's assistance is generally unwanted. A car stops; immediately the people collect, the breakdown gang push their way through, and in a few minutes the trouble is no more. Minoia's front axle was actually changed in a matter of 17 minutes. At prearranged stages a halt is made to refill. The drivers leap out, perhaps have a quick wash while their opponents roar past outside, eat, drink, learn the state of the race and rush off again. Victory is of the greatest importance, as it determines the make of car that shall be most in vogue for the ensuing season; the competition and anxiety are tremendous, especially when foreign makes challenge the Italians.

When I was thinking of taking part in this race in a British car, the people showed me much kindness, offering to arrange for my refuelling along the whole course. While the Alfa-Romeos were so eager to prove their own make the best in the world, or better than mine, that in the most sporting way they put their works entirely at my disposal. I was very sorry not to have been able to enter.

No wonder the publicity, financial aid and patronage which Italy showers on motor racing should have produced the finest driver living at the moment. This is Nuvolari; he is small, swarthy, dark and agitated, with all the fire of his southern blood in his veins. He does not have a fit of nerves before a race, but is wildly excited instead, and after it he is very modest, but still as excited. His record is amazing; he has won almost every big race in the world. Practice, which he gets weekly in the racing at Monza where he is much in demand, has brought him very near perfection, and I think to fling his car round corners as he does and keep it on the road against all adverse conditions, his wrists and forearms must be made of steel. He laps at terrific speed, and is the opposite of his fellow, Borzacchini, a steady, very fine driver, to whom the role of playing a waiting game is usually allotted.

The French crowds vie in hysteria with the Italian, without showing the same technical curiosity. They come from all regions of France to their big races, and their favours are influenced profoundly by patriotism and national rivalry. They exhort the Bugattis and Delages at the top of their voice, and, when one of their opponents is unfortunate, give tongue to the satisfaction which more shamefaced people keep concealed. They choose their idol almost as much for personal charm as skill in driving, and set him on an unassailable pinnacle. Their interest none the less, though founded on less mechanical knowledge than the German or Italian, is an intelligent one, and their tracks among the finest to be found. With Le Mans you should now be well acquainted. In the south there is the road course at Pau, where at a later date I had an exciting race in a four-seater Bentley. Montlhéry combines a road and track; the French Grand Prix was held this year at Rheims; on the coast are the Dieppe, Boulogne and Marseilles circuits, and elsewhere a number smaller, while in Belgium there is, of course, a season of good racing at Spa.

The Belgians are enthusiastic, with strong French sympathies. Both crowds are unanimous in their idolisation of Louis Chiron.

Chiron is the Beau Brummel; he accentuates an aristocratic appearance by immaculate dress and contempt of nerves. I have never seen his calm so much as ruffled, and with all his good looks, courtesy and attraction, he remains with every justification unchallenged master of French racing.

Most enthusiastic of all are the Ulster people. They know little about a car's anatomy, they go for the thrills; they love speed - Bentleys are especially popular. They congregate at the worst bends to see the skidding, and, for all this, have the most sympathy with the drivers, decrying bad work, cheering skill and bravery, commiserating with misfortune. They are, in short, the most sportsmanlike. The organisation of the Tourist Trophy races is an example of all that organising should be, and their Ulster police have been extolled with praise so high that they would no doubt prefer it left there.

The Dublin crowds could not be more different from those at Belfast. Considering their equal ignorance, I think they must be the most phlegmatic in the world.

There is, as far as I can see, no representative English crowd. Brooklands has its habitués, a little coterie whose attentions are for little else than mechanical matters. They are deeply interested, but very rarely moved, and to accuse them of waiting for thrills would be an unthinkable affront. Quite often a sprinkling of people of fashion drift to Brooklands, but though delightful ignorance might lead them to a display of emotion, aristocratic reserve forbids it.

There are no other circuits in England, road or track, of first-class importance, and the comparison of Brooklands to the group of two or three courses with which other countries are provided, is inadequate.

Organisation of racing in most countries is true to a very high standard, though a few foreign tracks are a prey to amateurish officials, whose only equipment against trouble is a whistle. The chief agent is the International Federation, most French races being managed by the French Club Automobile, the Italian by the Italian Club Automobile, and so on. Le Mans makes a remarkable exception. The meeting is launched by the now famous Automobile Club de l'Ouest, little more than a local club with a lively initiative, whose headquarters are at Le Mans.

The English are entertained royally everywhere, but only at Le Mans, which became almost a Bentley Dominion, are they regarded as serious competitors. Of this I shall have far more to say. In Grand Prix events, for racing cars, we are hardly considered. It is not a question of unpopularity at all, the foreigners would be only too glad for us to join the lists, but where is the car on which to enter? When I drove at Pau in my four-seater Bentley with its touring body and finished second, the French were so delighted to see one Englishman, even in a touring car among racing models, that they gave me the most unexpected applause. It was so rare an occasion.

The foreign drivers and mechanics, and all who have to do with race or management, make up the cheeriest of crowds, and at our first meeting we form a friendship revived at nearly every big event. Differences of language and contradictory political or religious sympathies make no odds; we are an unofficial fraternity, and both before and during the race help each other as much as the limits of competition allow. Afterwards one generally asks some of them to dinner at one's hotel, or dines with them at theirs, and there is no trace of envy or ill-feeling in any one. Our conversation might bore some people, but it does not bore us, and, but for the two hours on the mark and the possibility of an accident, the week is perfect.

— CHAPTER V —

1928

It is on the cards that this will be rather a dull chapter; it contains nothing but accounts of races in brief, and sketches of people at length. It would, however, have been tedious to give all my races the same space and labour that is devoted to the most important, so I have allowed only a passing mention to some, recalling the incidents for which they were most remarkable and disdaining a continuous story. It is not a question of deficient thrills, but of time and the reader's patience, for even my friends, who will, I hope, pester their libraries with demands for the book, may grow tired of monotonous description, and long for a little frivolity.

Of the Nürburg race in 1928 I have already said a little. We were hopelessly outclassed in the unsupercharged Bentleys by the giant supercharged Mercs. I finished eighth and was congratulated on all sides for my car's performance. The chairman of the Mercedes Company said that its running was so accurate and its lapping so regular, that people almost set their watches by it. To the German mind such precision had a particular appeal, and I treasure the memory of that event among my most precious.

One of its chief diversions had almost slipped my mind. Before the start, a commotion was observed among the great crowd, as if someone was trying to get through and finding it hard. Gradually the throngs parted, as down the lane of inquisitive Germans came a wonderful golden car, and in it reclined, like a Roman Emperor in Rome's most apolaustic days, the creator in person, none other than the great, the sublime Ettore Bugatti. It was indeed to be a big event, when the Golden Bug attended it.

Shortly afterwards the International Tourist Trophy was first held on the Ards circuit in Belfast. It aroused great excitement in the neighbourhood and interest elsewhere, for was this not the first great British event since the Isle of Man T.T. in 1922, and only the third since the Gordon Bennett Cup in 1903. The most distinguished foreign drivers announced their intention of competing, seven nations were to be represented, and at last the old empire was pulling herself together. Of course, it was a pity one had to go to Ireland to see Englishmen driving English cars, but there were the laws, there were the peace and quiet of the English public to be considered. So over the Irish Channel everyone went, most of them rather sick on the way, and arrived to find Ulster *en fête*.

I think some thousands of pounds had been spent on the organisation, and two thousand policemen drilled for weeks, to control a crowd capable of anything when agitated. But the race, like all others of the kind, was not being held solely to send shivers down the backs of pretty colleens. Only standard cars that had been catalogued by February 29th were permitted, and figures of sales had to be shown that there might be no doubt of their commercial purpose. This was no jaunt for freaks, but a serious experiment, a test of makes, a criterion of national industries. Any fuel not at the disposal of the public in ordinary filling stations was unconditionally forbidden.

The Newtownards circuit is thirteen miles and two-thirds long. It is shaped like a kite, with three famous corners known by the names of their villages, Newtownards itself, Comber, and the worst of all, the hairpin at Dundonald, which is approached by a straight of about 1½ miles. The danger here, both to buildings and spectators, is so great that strong barricades were erected and warnings issued. Thirty laps had to be completed for a total run of 410 miles, but a number of laps, varying with the engine capacity, was credited to each car as handicap, those of over 3000 c.c. starting at scratch, and the 747c.c. Austins with 5 laps, which left them only 25 to finish.

A sensation was caused by the withdrawal from the race of the official Bentley team, whose views this system did not suit. The Mercedes team also withdrew, owing to a regulation about the number of spare wheels which might be carried. But I kept my own Bentley in, and Scrap Thistlethwayte his own

Mercedes, though at the eleventh hour I was forced to spend about a hundred pounds in deference to the following strange rule. It was decreed that the front cushion of the back seat should be one foot and seven inches distant from the back of the front seat. This is almost unattainable in a sports car. In the old 3-litre Bentleys the distance was one foot two inches, and they had been long in popular use, and regarded as standard models. In the 4½-litre it was one foot six inches, and in the Le Mans Lagondas one foot four inches. My car had been passed for racing under the rules of the Association Internationale des Automobile Club Reconnus, a body with an influence as far spread as its name, and it seemed as if the Belfast authorities were carrying their efficiency too far. For by demanding this change, they altered the whole car, and, as the change made it no longer standard in this one respect, they could not strictly describe it as a standard model.

Malcolm Campbell in a Bugatti, Kaye Don in a Lea-Francis were to continue their Brooklands' duels on the Ards course, and Lord Curzon, as he then was, was to drive a Bugatti. But the idol of the Crowd was Scrap Thistlethwayte, whose good looks, and possibly the attraction of being described as a millionaire, made him the victim of the ladies. He was so often besieged by the much-advertised and charming Belfast girls that it was thought a newspaper had hired them for the purpose. On the bonnet of his white Mercedes was a silk stocking, which went round the course at the lap record of 72 mph. Thistlethwayte is a good and very fast driver, but has not raced for over two years.

The practice runs gave every excuse for expecting extremely high speeds, and there was one bad accident. C. S. Bell in a Riley approaching Quarry Corner at 90 mph, skidded and dashed into, a hedge. The car overturned twice and he, with his mechanic, were flung out into a field. They were naturally a little shaken, but unhurt.

I was driving my 4½-litre Bentley with Bernard Rubin as relief driver, and the Black Hawk Stutz of Le Mans was also committed, hungry for revenge. A Frenchman, Vassena, had entered a Tracta, but boarded the wrong boat at Liverpool and went to the Isle of Man, so the officials waived the practice rules and he was allowed to start. In this they showed a lenient attitude that might with advantage be more often adopted, though, on the whole, the staff at Belfast managed their first job admirably.

The race lived up to the expectations of the crowd, and the Belfast girls felt their spines shiver more than once. There were some terrible crashes, Clive Gallop skidding into a telegraph pole, and his mechanic being hurled several yards. This happened soon after Ballystockart Bridge, the telegraph pole came down in half, and Clive was found, serene but astonished, in mid-air while the car stood on its nose. The mechanic was winded.

But not all ended in comedy. During the early laps there was a disaster in which not the most callous could find a laugh.

I was driving behind Malcolm Campbell. We were both going very fast, and as he began to slow down to go into the pits, I saw little flames shooting out beneath his petrol tank. He stopped, and at that very moment the whole car went ablaze; clouds of black smoke poured from the exhaust, mingling with the fire. People ran out with extinguishers, but they could not make any impression or even move the car off the course as it had been left in gear. As I rushed by, the smoke blew into my eyes, and I could see nothing, but had a vague idea that people were on the course and very near me. I went straight by, missing some, so I heard later, by inches, and when I came round on the next lap, the car was already a skeleton, with the flames still licking its sides and spreading a tremendous heat. Malcolm Campbell was watching it in utter dejection, as the smoke died down and left a furnace of boiling ashes where the cockpit had been. He had entertained high hopes for the race and done very well in practice. Worst of all, the car was not insured, and I believe its loss cost him more than a thousand pounds.

Soon afterwards the Bentley developed oil trouble and I pulled in to mend a broken oil-pipe, but I could not catch up the smaller cars with their big handicaps. Still, it would be ungenerous to complain when I finished fifth and actually averaged the highest speed, of 65.76 mph. It was a fine effort of the Bentley's, when at one time there was an ugly smell of burning oil, and grey smoke coming through its bonnet. But the day was divided between Leon Cushman in his Alvis and Kaye Don in his Lea-Francis; they both had handicaps of 3 laps, were both very skilful drivers, and had a wonderful fight for first place. On the twenty-sixth lap, Cushman, who was then 10 seconds only behind Don, skidded badly and lost 25 more; on the final lap Don was leading by 26, but Cushman began to catch him and the two came down the incline at the finish close together. Don just got home by 13 seconds. There were 13 cars in his class, and his time was 5 hours 58 minutes and 13 seconds.

A fine race was run by Lord Curzon, who drove with great skill for 150 miles at nearly 68 m.p.h. and after that averaged over seventy. He had at half distance overtaken all the one-lap handicap cars, and was gaining every second on the very smallest, with a good chance of victory, when his petrol tank burst, as had Malcolm Campbell's, and he was forced to give up. He had there, as everywhere, a marked popularity with the crowd, and drove superbly. Before the race his signature was much sought, and given, to autograph albums, and he held a small levée round his car for schoolboys and politicians. He has said so much about me in his foreword, that I shall now have no mercy on him.

After taking a degree at almost every police court in the land, he decided to practise his speed where it would be more appreciated, and exact from the constabulary of the track a licence they had refused him on main roads. This was in 1928. In four years he has managed to acquire the reputation and experience of a veteran, carving out for himself a position in which he is unique. Under an uncommon gaiety, for which he is justly popular on all courses, is a serious devotion to motoring which goes far beyond mere words. He has been associated with most recent stages in its advance, and is continually impressing on the public the importance of racing to the motor industry. He is the Borotra of the track. Always distinguishable by brilliant blue overalls and helmet, under a huge Oxford blue umbrella he becomes a landmark in the rain, and at Montlhéry he sat in his car with it up until a few seconds before the start.

Of all racing motorists with whom I have ever come in contact, he is, I think, the keenest. He brings to any subject with which cars are remotely connected an application that nothing will deter. In his own runs, he is the first to be on the course and the last to leave it, never content until he has learnt every bump, every twist or pothole by heart - a genius indeed, if genius be, as is said, the infinite capacity for taking pains. His own enthusiasm has given him a sharp eye for keenness in others. There is nobody more eager to assist the sincere novice and many is the time he has taken, as his spare drivers in big events, men whose racing ambitions had not the same scope to fulfil themselves as his own. But most of all he is a patriot. It is his great hope to find an English car good enough for Continental races, and when it is found, to drive it. He is censured by the sort of people whom ignorance makes critical for not driving his own country's cars, but he is only longing to do so if one can be produced worth driving. He has a passion for the cleanliness of his machines, and believes rightly that an unkempt appearance will hamper their prestige and tarnish their country's reputation. So all his cars arrive at the start sleek, with every spot removed, and the full possible advantage squeezed out of polish.

His skill and bravery are household words, and if the ship of state were a car, Lord Howe would have been Prime Minister long ago.

September saw my last big race in 1928, which was held on the Boulogne road course for the Georges Boillot Cup. Twelve laps of the 23 mile circuit had to be completed, under handicaps still based on cubic capacity, and awarded not by laps but by time.

So, in my 4½-litre Bentley of Le Mans and Ulster, I was giving 28 minutes 36 seconds to the Lea-Francises, and 1 hour 5 minutes to the little Amilcars that started first. The team of Alfa-Romeos, which had swept the board in Italy and Belgium, was entered and also the old Black Hawk Stutz, still hungry for revenge. Malcolm Campbell was driving another Bugatti while a certain racer of note had decided to partake, but met with fraternal disapproval on grounds of business connection. He refused to pay any attention. They stormed, they pleaded, they pointed out the dangers; he was adamant. But in the night, while no one was guarding the car, the man's brother, imbued with noble principles, stole into the garage, a hammer in his hand, and with a few strong blows through the radiator, settled the matter for both sides.

The day before the race Malcolm Campbell broke the lap record at 78.12 miles per hour, and in the race itself was obviously out for victory. He drove magnificently, and took something off his handicap at every turn; fourth in the third lap, third in the fifth, he was leading in the eighth. My Bentley was running perfectly, but I saw it would be impossible to catch up on an hour's start in a race that only lasted four hours. I had one unpleasant moment, when the car was running downhill at about 80 and skidded on to the grass. There was forest at either side, and I actually tore away the small bushes on its fringe. I was able to go on, but the race was between Campbell and the Frenchman Dutilleux, both of whom were driving Bugattis. On the eighth lap, with three more to go, Campbell gained 40 seconds, but found that his brakes were beginning to fail. At one corner he skidded up a bank and flew about six feet through the air, but on the ninth he was three minutes ahead. Approaching a bend, he found that the brakes had gone completely, and his gears being unequal to the strain of stopping the car, he dashed up a side road towards Boulogne. After this he had to retire, and the victory seemed assured to Dutilleux. His friends were waiting for him with huge bouquets, when two miles from the finish he took a corner too fast, skidded, and lost a wheel, escaping injury himself by a stroke of luck. Behind were a Salmson, and Ivanowsky in one of the Alfas. Seeing that the race was now between them, they came furiously up the straight. Ivanowsky passed a little way from the finish, and got home by a few seconds.

In this and in the Belfast race it seemed inevitable that one of two cars must win. In both, too, there was a great fight, but at Belfast between the two expected, and here between two who had hardly been considered. The two Bugattis, in their keenness to win, defeated each other's object, and neither finished. The Salmson was second, and "Salmson a L'honneur" proclaimed a French journalist, but I think not. The honour was due to the team of Alfa-Romeos, who finished in the first, third, and fourth places, giving a foretaste of their future triumphs and British disappointments.

The winner, Ivanowsky, does not make his last appearance on this page. He is a tall, fine-looking Russian, an ex-officer of the Russian Army, and, so I have been told, escaped death in the Revolution by about twenty minutes.

It should be worth while giving some short account of the controversy that stormed around the withdrawal of the Bentley team from the T.T. race. It is understood that a team races to advertise its products for the benefit of the public. It would, therefore, be unfair to arrange handicaps that excluded a particular firm from so much as a glimpse of victory. Yet such arrangements were made by the Belfast officials in 1928, not, of course, on purpose, but under the influence of false judgment. The smaller cars were credited with such a number of laps, the course is so ill adapted to continued passing, and passing would be necessary so often to the big Bentleys, that they could not possibly have won, or run into a place. They therefore retired, in deference to their own tradition of good prominence in all their events, and also to their shareholders, preferring to take no part at all than be content with a back seat. For this they had good reasons, which in a private entrant would lose their point, as he has no publicity to consider for his car and no shareholders to satisfy.

Yet certain ill-informed backbiters saw fit to impute this withdrawal of the Bentleys to cowardice, hinting that they were intended for the track and had done nothing of note upon the road. This, in face of Le Mans, in face of Montlhéry, in face of Le Mans once more! After a short while, the issue was side-tracked into profitless digressions and sententious moralising, and closed with the honour of the Bentleys vindicated.

There can be no praise allowed this firm, without recalling the man whose name it bears, W. O. Bentley, or to give him the title by which he is best known, W. O. He is the finest team manager I have ever driven under; he controls his cars as if they were toy trains and he manoeuvring them with levers in the pits.

He moves them forward or pulls them back at will, by a special arrangement of signals, and God help the driver who disobeys him. For W. O., in ordinary conversation quiet and oysterlike, has as sharp an edge to his tongue as a piqued prima donna. He is quite impassive; if a team of 20 of his most glorious cars either came in in the first 20 places, or crashed in the first 20 minutes, he would be equally unruffled, and yet he has a generous nature and gives more help to the drivers who want it than any other man in the sport. On those who ask sincerely for his aid, he bestows it without resting, and in return his word is law, his frown almost a social barrier to its recipients, and his smile something to live on for days.

So 1928 went out. In his Blue Bird Malcolm Campbell had broken the world's speed record, with an average of 206 m.p.h., which Ray Keech raised again in the same year to 207. At Le Mans the Bentleys had triumphed and at Belfast, Kaye Don. Mrs. Strickland had crossed on her Star 7,236 miles of desert, through jungle and sand, in 58 days of actual running. And with these English names ringing in its ears and Sir Henry Segrave making ready to regain the world's record for England, the year departed, and 1929 came in.

— CHAPTER VI —

The Dirty Work

I cannot set my pen to this chapter without apologising for a serious omission. I have made a point of commending all those in general, from whom deserved praise is withheld, without mentioning a particular name. The man who has been responsible for most of the preparation of my cars, to whom more credit is due than I dare estimate, remains unspecified. Clive Gallop's part in my racing career is as unobtrusive as it is invaluable. He has done all the hardest work in a cramped repair shop, pored by night over his calculations, called himself to account for failure. His knowledge of a car's career, from its genesis to the moment the flag falls on the start, is without an equal. Yet to the world at large his name is almost unknown. He is far more competent to write this section than I, who therefore dedicate my own account in humility and gratitude to him.

The driver of a racing car may become excellent, but he cannot become perfect. By unrelenting hard work extended over many years, which gives him a thoroughly intimate and almost infallible knowledge of his machine, he reaches a rung in the ladder beyond which it is impossible to climb. But it is not the topmost rung; this is barred to him by the weakness and unreliability of his own flesh. He may be able to exact from his car a speed which mathematicians have proved to be beyond defeat, that cannot be exceeded by an infinitesimal fraction of a second, and he may have mastered an angle on all his corners which can never be narrowed without disaster, but the irregularities of his own nature, always stronger than he, will leave him short of the goal of perfection. He has no means of preventing a sudden fit of apoplexy or a momentary blurring of sight, and as long as this impotence to control every circumstance continues, which presumably will be for ever, perfection is out of his reach.

But it is not out of the reach of his car; and here let me explain, that I use the word "perfect," not of infinite speed in golden chariots, but in the ordinary sense of utter reliability, the finest construction, and a speed only sufficient to win all big races. Of these a car is capable. For it is not liable to the contagion of disease, which a man finds impossible to ignore; every one of its members is independent, and can be examined, investigated and finally perfected without the fear of outside interruption. If a mechanic catches cold, the plugs do not begin to sneeze; they wait, aloof from the unforeseen perils of humanity, for the last touch that puts them beyond improvement. A car in the making has no life of its own until it is completed, and can therefore give no check to its perfection but a driver has too much life of his own, and too many eccentricities of health and emotion, for his skill ever to be considered quite dependable. I think that a car is unique in thus being empowered to reach a stage more advanced than other instruments of sport, whether they be human or not. It cannot be led astray by a private whim. The driver may have a sudden desire to drive into a wall or to give up a race from boredom, but the car is not capable of boredom nor sensible of desires. A boxer may have a faultless physique, with a perfect command of his art, and ruin his chances by drunkenness or nerves on the day of the fight, but a car has no nerves and is unable to drink. There is no positive guarantee against a horse falling down dead in the middle of the course, when it appeared sound in wind and limb, but the collapse of a car can be made impossible by the diligence of its mechanics. It has no weaknesses, no humours, no life developed of its own accord. That it has a life I maintain as strongly as I did at the beginning; but it is illusory, an impression of life, the life of a thing that breathes, but has no reactions or emotions. It is a robot. It can be made to do anything, but is powerless without human aid. So when I feel the harmony stirring between myself and my car, I know that I have given power to something that did not before have that power, but neither did it have my weaknesses. It is not liable to fail suddenly owing to a weak heart or fatigue. Its failures are due to the ignorance of the driver or the bad preparation of the mechanic. The latter may neglect an essential detail, or the former unduly stress the engine. Either is capable of carelessness. But if carelessness is barred by the most unwearying labour and strictness, the car has the material to put itself beyond criticism. The chassis is there, the wheels, the tyres, the engine, everything is there, unresisting, untrammelled by mortal anxieties, waiting all for that perfection of which some have already been shown capable.

Some three or four weeks before the race the trouble begins, and from then onwards there is a ceaseless round of inspection, revision and innovation. The smallest details are subjected to an exhaustive scrutiny, which may reveal still smaller details needing improvement inside them, and each mechanic is allotted his particular responsibility. At the outset, the whole car is stripped for thorough examination like an army recruit, and a note made of anything out of date or insecure. As a good mechanic is sure to find one of these failings, if not both, in every portion of chassis and engine, it is some time before this stage is passed. Provided the design is good, very little difficulty is involved apart from the concentration and hard work; only knowledge and common sense are required to notice what is in need of change or repair, and these are qualities for which mechanics are especially chosen. There exists certain problems – some of them lately solved – which are invariably chalked up before any actual dismantling takes place, problems of tyres and no satisfactory elucidation has yet appeared. The temperature to which it is raised in fast cars is terrific, and the comparison of its heat to the heat in ordinary touring cars, like a comparison between the Italian and German crowds, one over boiling point and the other at normal.

When the first ailments have been treated, the car is taken over a track for three or four hundred miles at a slow speed, and in the event of success on this jousting ground, transported without more ado to the field of battle. But the event of success is so rare that more dismantling usually follows the first practice. Before the Dublin race in 1930 we were dissatisfied in this way, and found that the meshes of the steel radiator guard were set too close. So during the night of Wednesday, in order to have the car ready to regulations on Thursday, the mechanics worked, without sleep, cutting away every third wire, and reducing the compression ratio of the engine. There were never less than eight men busy at a time; along the benches lay any tools that might be needed, and whenever one man left his place there was another waiting to take it. When morning came, the electric lights were still flaring in the workshop and the finishing touches on the point of being added; but even then there was no rest for the workers until the car was safely on its journey to Ireland.

On the evening or afternoon before the race, there is a final inspection, when everyone is in a strained state of nerves about his own contribution. It is far more serious than any preparation for a battle. On the eve of Waterloo there was a ball, but the eve of Belfast or Le Mans sees a score of garages full of weary men in filthy overalls, drawing out oil, clearing filters, checking valve clearances, ignition, and valve springs, and endeavouring to reassure themselves that they at least have done everything within their power. Then the car is presented to the driver. He has it filled up with oil and petrol and water, like the Lord breathing into the Valley of Dry Bones, sees that the spare parts are collected and the wheels balanced, and an hour or two before the race brings it on to the course. After waiting for another three-quarters of an hour, he warms up the engine until he is satisfied, and substitutes a new set of tested plugs. At Belfast in 1930, engines had to be stopped a quarter of an hour before the flag fell, and the self-starter used to start them. But in Grand Prix events for stripped racing cars, they are left running. They must not be running too fast, the throttle must not be opened too wide as the driver lets out the clutch, or the engine may be choked or the clutch slip. But usually every man is sitting in his car waiting, with the clutch already held out.

Away goes the driver; but this is not a signal for the mechanics to have a good sleep and then settle down to a free view from the grandstand. They have already taken up their position in the pits.

These are not large holes dug in the ground to hide the various opponents, but a row of hutches by the side of the road, whither the cars come to refuel and do their repairs. Each team has the pits for its cars in one place, and on either side those of its rivals. Along the front there runs a counter where everything that may be of use to the driver is put in readiness. There is seldom much noise or bustle in the English quarter, but the foreigners have not the same calm, the Italians especially giving their agitation tongue without shame. At one time far too many people were allowed in; anyone who knew someone who knew a relation of a driver would ask a party of friends, as if it were to a box at a music-hall, but that has changed in recent years. There are generally three cars, for which the following are needed in the pits to the exclusion of all others: an engine mechanic, who has been in charge of all the preparation, a chassis man, at the Le Mans races an electrician for the batteries, and four timekeepers to clock the cars at each lap. There would also be two "floating mechanics," one of whom is in charge of the food and drink, and about five or six outside make sure that the right mixtures of benzol and petrol are used, and the petrol poured from the tins into huge four-gallon churns. These are placed on the counter when the time for refuelling is due; great care has to be exercised in tipping them into the petrol tank. The driver, whose job it is, would come in dazed after the strain of a long drive, and probably spill petrol on to the exhaust or splash it into his own eyes. This latter I have never yet done, partly because experience has warned me against its dangers, and partly because I have a habit of fixing my mind on events some minutes ahead, and am so prepared. But wherever it has happened, the unlucky driver has been in agony for at least five minutes, and precious time has been wasted before he could continue. The trouble with the exhaust caused a bad accident to my mechanic, Chevrollier, which shall be duly related in its proper sequence.

In supreme control of the whole team is, surprisingly enough, the team manager. In his hands the cars, the drivers and the mechanics are like marionettes. His word is law, and his position that of a commander-in-chief; the entire organisation of the team is in his hands, the choice of policy and the jockeying of his cars into place for the final effort. Days before he begins to make up his mind about the tactics to adopt; he has to read between the lines of rumour, deduce from his own men's times, and compare them with the times of others. He is in a position of implicit trust; no fair vamp must dig his secrets from him; his heart must be of stout English oak to guard his country's honour. He can say what he likes, on the invariable and respected understanding that it is not brought up against him after the race, and with a company of men in a touchy humour he has every opportunity. Complete obedience to the team manager is essential, and personalities, especially in an amateur team, must be subordinated. I have offended against this law more than once myself, for which there is no excuse, except the usual and unsatisfactory one of nerves. At Le Mans, the year I passed Carraciola with the threads of a tyre flying, we had fitted 1¼-inch steel mudguard stays which were enormously strong. But when the tread began to fly, they were bent like little pieces of wire. In the morning Chassagne was about to hand the car over to me, the sun was very hot, and I put on a white pique racing helmet instead of a crash helmet. Bertie Moir said that I was not going to drive in that, with the mudguards hardly covering the wheels and every chance of a piece of tread flying up and hitting me on the back of the head. I said that I was going to wear it, and had no intention of changing. Chassagne was due in less than a minute. Bertie Moir said that I was going to put on the crash helmet. I said that Bertie Moir could go to a hotter place than Le Mans. Chassagne was approaching the pits. Bertie Moir replied that he would go there after I had put on the crash helmet. We were both tired, but managed to fling a few expressive insults. We then suddenly found that there was something ludicrous in the situation, and as Chassagne drew in I put on the crash helmet and took my place. The more we recall that incident, the more we laugh at it; no suspicion of ill-will ever rankled over it. I do not believe Bertie Moir could harbour any ill-will if he tried for a week.

But his duties as team manager do not end with calming the troubled spirits of his drivers; he has to wake some of them out of the stupor in which they reach the pits, and force them to do their refuelling as quickly as possible or discover if they have any trouble that needs attention. He told me that he actually saw Leo d'Erlanger pull up, let his car go on fire, and sit among the flames, like Brünnhilde, until he could collect his wits to realise that wise men would jump out.

The team manager has to start at least two or three months before the race, collecting everything that will be needed in the pits: fillers, funnels, oil, signals and all the cumbersome paraphernalia that are under his charge, and not only is he responsible for these, together with a museum of jugs, pots, flags, nuts, bolts, screws, but also for an infallible knowledge of the rules of racing. These vary disconcertingly with the different courses, and their variety, though interesting to the lay mind, is a plague to the team manager. At Le Mans one year we had to run with wings, windscreens and wireguards all of a certain size, while at Ulster we had no wings, lamps or windscreens at all, and wind deflectors were optional. In the 1930 Grand Prix, mechanics were allowed to fill up and change wheels, but in the T.T. only the driver and the mechanic on the car; and at Le Mans the two drivers were the only people allowed to do the refuelling and any necessary repairs. These are only a very few of the more prominent differences in regulation. There are a myriad more dealing with far minuter details.

Through this ocean of difficulties the team manager has to wade unbewildered. He is also in control of the signals which are thrust out as the driver passes, giving him other instructions of policy, or information from the official judges, or news of the other cars nearest him in the running. Bertie Moir used to arrange that the radiator of the car drew up opposite the pit manager's flag, where all the oil and waterjugs would be placed, while the petrol funnel and petrol churns were a little farther down the counter, aligned with the tank; by this method 25 or 30 seconds could be gained, a large fraction of the time spent in refuelling. Perfect calm is essential for a fast refill, which has often been known to change the aspect of a race. During my struggle with Carraciola we were both due at the pits, and if I could gain 30 seconds, we would be level for the next lap. He took 2 minutes 35 seconds, and was just too quick for us, who took 2 minutes 15 seconds. An average refill of 38-40 gallons lasted from 1 minute 50 seconds to 2 minutes 10 seconds. In the T.T. race we calculated on a rate of seven miles to a gallon and always put in 34 gallons at the start, but half-way through we used to fill up again to give us a certain non-stop run if the race became close at the finish. Our record wheel-change was 31 seconds. But I think that if I had to change a wheel on a main thoroughfare, I should probably take half an hour.

I hold the opinion that the very greatest drivers are born and not made, though unwearying application and invincible patience may ultimately set a man in the forefront with those who reached it by the easy stages of genius. But he must start young and devote everything in him to it, if only first-class honours can content his ambition. I remember a little while ago that a young Cambridge undergraduate came up and confided in me his secret wish to win the Inter-Varsity trials. He said that he had several fast cars, but did not know how to drive them, I forget if he called me "Sir" - that I consented to do what I could, and off we went in one of his cars on a fast strip of road. He fired off volleys of the most intelligent questions, which displayed a disarming ignorance that I did my best to correct. I had the satisfaction of seeing him flushed and excited with victory after his race, and though he was not able to stop at the end and crashed through a fence and a hedge into a field, that lad definitely showed the right spirit. He is now quite a good driver.

There is at Brooklands no professional on whose bosom the would-be driver can fling himself; but there are skilled amateurs who will go out of their way to fill the gap. It is in this that Sir Henry Segrave rendered such ceaseless and invaluable service to motoring, and his mantle has fallen upon Lord Howe. They have encouraged the novice by personal action better than honeyed words; they have taken him in their cars both in their spare time and during a race, and thereby given him the best elementary training he could find. The best school of motoring is in the cockpit by the side of the expert, to which the entrance examination is a brief question - are you keen, are you serious, or do you just want an experience to boast about? If you can give a satisfactory answer and are fortunate enough to find a skilled driver with the leisure to drive you, and a car that has run previously in big events, make the best of a wonderful opportunity. Mark where the driver goes through each particular trick; at this tree he lifts his foot for a corner, opposite that bridge begins to brake really hard, here he changes down, there he starts to turn the wheel. Stamp into your mind the corners where he swerves out, and the others to which he clings, and impress ineradicably the number of engine revolutions at which he changes from top to third and from third to second. If your luck is thoroughly in and he does several laps, take his lap speeds and absorb them as you absorbed the alphabet, and if you have made all these a part of you, acquiring at least a certain knowledge of what not to do, you may then be permitted to take the wheel yourself. At first it will feel strange, and the car remind you of an unruly horse, alarming, with more than a suggestion of bolting. But do not attempt to hitch your wagon to the star who first drove it; leave yourself a wider margin of safety, while imitating faithfully the sequence of his movements. Drive slower, brake sooner, and at the corners keep your revolutions two or three hundred below his. Presently will come the first stirrings of confidence, born not out of Trusting to Luck by Pious Hope, but emerging gradually from patience and denial of rash impulses.

To have experienced this is to have travelled half-way to success. You may then begin to increase your speed, to take your corners faster and wait longer to brake, and to compare your own laps with his.

I cannot exaggerate the importance of this familiarity, confidence and ease to the young driver. It makes impossible what is inexcusable, harsh gear-changing, and broadside skidding at corners. These crimes are the sign of what is branded as a "handfisted" driver. It is as essential for a racing motorist to have "hands" as it is for a good jockey.

The path of success, even though covered in a car, is a thoroughly uncomfortable one to a refined nature. But refinement and shrinking from troubles are not the qualities of a great driver. He, and those who wish to emulate him, have to undergo a physical strain beyond the imagination of the lay mind. They face the agony of jolting for hours on end, and often the pain of serious injury, while many of their races leave them in a state of utter exhaustion. They are met with misunderstanding, disappointment, disillusion and severe criticism from those they benefit; they have to rise superior to popular apathy and even definite discouragement. Yet, if they can endure these trials, devoting their attention to learning their job alone, they will profit by their experience and approach the fulfilment of their hopes.

The ardour of the novice must never run away with him. In practice he must be patient with corners that continue to baffle him. The car will not be forced to do anything; it must be wheedled and coaxed into submission. Reliable driving is the only way by which to ensure safety and success. It is not only the driver who is concerned, but all the other competitors in the race. His consideration of them must never, under any pretext, on any occasion, be submerged. Those who sin in this respect generally fail to complete the course, and always run the gauntlet of universal odium. They are not offered cars; their company becomes unpleasant; their team is ashamed of them, and, if they do not mend their ways, gets rid of them for good. There is no need for underhand subtlety. No Carraciola, or Nuvolari, or Chiron, has ever been indebted to even a shadow of unfair means. In the whole history of motor racing, very, very few great drivers have been suspected of spitefulness or dishonesty; and those that have, soon found that the notoriety of their methods overshadowed the fame of their success. There is no question of the opportunity to cheat. The more skilled the driver, the easier he would find it. He could deny a pursuing car sufficient room to overtake, or make a show of giving it and suddenly swing out; he could attempt to cut in unfairly on the wrong side of the course, and commit crimes by design which the novice commits by accident. But sooner or later he will meet his Waterloo. He will find himself pitted against a good and determined driver who nips his idiosyncrasies in the bud, and ends him, likely enough, in the ditch which he deserves.

— CHAPTER VII —

1929

I have now thrown on the screen, in four different events, four different pictures of the sport. People are found to complain of monotony, who can interpret the spectacle of a race only as a recurrence, at intervals, of noisy cars, all of them exactly alike and tiresomely repugnant to taking risks. They insist that there is no variety and little humour, while "as for edification, we cannot be put to so much trouble and research to discover it." But if they could do me the favour of considering these four 1928 races, a curious dissimilarity of character might reveal itself.

At Le Mans I was the victim of disaster, which so far from turning the day into a disappointment, led ultimately to a wild and successful race against time. At Nürburg I enjoyed to my heart's content the pleasures of a wonderful course, a sympathetic crowd and a car running to perfection. At Ulster, the spectators had the thrill of a close finish, and myself the honour of the fastest time. At Boulogne, the palm went to an outsider, after unimagined failures by the two hot favourites. In all these races there were the usual skids, crashes and bouleversements, a fund of sensations, and sufficient comedy to lighten what was tragic in each one. But the store of incident is as yet scarcely tapped, and in all of the following races a new adventure or a fresh touch of humour comes to my mind.

Spurred by the incentive of Le Mans, and awakening to the backwardness of British automobile clubs, in May 1929, the Brooklands officials decided to hold a new race. It was to last for twenty-four whole hours, and be confined to touring models adjusted slightly for the track. Substantial prizes would be offered, and presented by a person of distinction. Again, at last, the old country was pulling herself together. It was, of course, a pity that any comparison with Le Mans should be quite ridiculous, Le Mans being a road course very near perfection, and Brooklands an out-of-date track; and a greater pity that the chief glory of Le Mans, the driving through the night, could not be imitated, owing to the prejudices against noise of the people of Weybridge. This great new venture, this English Le Mans, was to consist of two days' racing of twelve hours each day, and on Friday evening at 8 o'clock the cars would be stopped, tucked up in a special garage, and locked in for the night. No change could be made to make their sleep more comfortable, and punctually at eight next morning out they would come to finish the race.

A distance, ranged in proportion to varying cubic capacities, had to be covered, the winner being the man who most exceeded it. Superchargers were also handicapped, to an extent equalling an extra 30 per cent, on the cubic capacity. The race was won by Ramponi in an Alfa-Romeo, two more of that team being third and fourth. So was the menace of foreign makers realised at the very outset of the new year.

There was some doubt about the victor, Sammy Davis's Bentley having passed the post quarter of a mile in front of Ramponi, but after much sliding of the official slide-rules, and confabulation of the big-wigs in the omnibus where they were ensconced, the Italian was proclaimed by a margin of .003 on the figure of merit, 3½ miles on handicap. It was in this race that Mrs. Chetwynd stopped a leak in the radiator with a wad of chewing gum, and a certain gentleman found that, if his car was built to regulation, his own thighbones were oversized. Only after the most fatiguing tug-of-war was he extracted from the cockpit. But these are not my foremost memories of the Double Twelve. It is linked, for me, with an accident which came very near to ending in tragedy.

The car had a special silencer of standard design with a fishtail of standard length projecting from the back. It was a rule that all the drivers should at once switch off their engines as they pulled up at the pits. When I came in to refill I switched off in obedience, but while going a little faster than usual, and gas collected in the silencer. My mechanic, Chevrollier, leapt out of the car, pushed the petrol funnel into the tank, and began to pour in one of the 4 gallon churns off the counter. As he did so, a little of the petrol fell on to his overalls, and, at the same instant, on to the exhaust. The unburnt charge in the silencer caught fire, and a wicked puff of flame shot out of the fishtail. In 30 seconds after the engine had stopped, Chevrollier was a blaze of flames. His wits were dazed after close on three hours in the car, and he began to walk with the empty churn to the pit counter. On it lay 32 gallons in open churns, ready to be put in, and only as he was almost touching them, and the fire burning up around his face and arms, did someone reach and push him aside, trying to make him collect his wits. But he did not know what he was doing, and began running down the pits, the flames rising higher. Somebody knocked him down, and then Rubin leapt across the pit counter with a Pyrene, shouting, "Shut your eyes." He sprayed his blazing overalls, and tried to roll him over and over on the ground, until at last the flames were out. But Chevrollier was terribly burnt, and a spare mechanic put straight into the car, which went off without delay. Never afterwards has any Bentley team gone to a race without a properly equipped fire-drill party of three mechanics, holding a damp blanket, two Pyrenes and some sand ready when the car comes in to refill, and Bertie Moir always throws a pail of cold water over the tail of the exhaust himself, thereby raising a huge cloud of hissing steam to the consternation of all uninitiated spectators.

Le Mans returned, and brought with it a Bentley victory so sweeping and monotonous that it became almost exciting. So much has been said of this occasion, it has been made the subject of such profound patriotic sentiment, that to rehearse its details in dull prose would be like talking a nursery rhyme. I have nearly a hundred press cuttings about it and can find no comparison except the Aga Khan's recent conquest of Doncaster and the National Party triumph in the last election. The finish must have been unforgettable to those who watched it; one after another, not two, not three, but four Bentleys sailed proudly up the straight, each in perfect line and distance behind the one preceding. My own, which I was driving with Babe Barnato, won without even giving the smallest intimation of trouble, and it was very seldom that any of the other three pulled in. Well might the French *Matin* complain of dullness! I shall not be surprised, if years hence Englishmen refer to Le Mans in 1929 to locate the heyday of their motor industry. There was never a suggestion of any other car passing ours. Such unique success was a marvel to those that partook of it, and lasting proof that whatever the future has in store, for a while at least, British racing cars have been the world's champions in these events.

Before taking over from Babe on one of our nightly changes, I asked him if the car needed anything, to which he answered, "Tighten up the shock-absorbers!" I took them up half a turn, and for an hour until they slackened, was more uncomfortable than I have ever been in my life. I was shaken and tossed and bounced and bruised and bumped, and came to my relay's end with but one desire, vengeance on Babe. I drew in to hand the car over, and warned him to tighten the shock-absorbers yet more. He took them up one whole turn, and I chuckled as he drove off in the highest of spirits. Whenever he passed, his face seemed to wear a strained look, and he returned a changed and broken man, with every bone in his body a living ache, and a fixed resolve to sit on nothing but the softest of chairs.

His driving that day was, as it always has been, an example of unselfishness. When I consider that we were in his own car, and that the sensation of four Bentleys led to triumph would find its way to the heart of an already moved audience, I wonder at the modesty with which he insisted on my taking our winner over the line, and the kindness of asking me to start the first laps, as he did that year. He is a great sportsman, and a fine athlete, a boxer, a horseman, but alas, no longer a racing driver. If his business had not forced him to give up racing, he would certainly have been in the topmost flight. W. O. watched the whole of the race without a sign of exultation, knowing from a long experience the powers of the eleventh hour. Even when it became obvious that two Bentleys at the very least must win, he made no display of his emotion. Somebody asked him, "What will happen if your cars fill the first four places?" and received no answer in words; but if looks can kill, W. O. murdered him.

Once more the Brooklands lists opened, this time upon the second round of the Anglo-Italian Tournament. Both 1½ and 2-litre Alfa-Romeos had entered, but without the aegis of an official team management, and their subsequent failure emphasised the popular conviction, that the obstacles in the way of separately run cars are nearly insuperable. The race was again to Barnato, in the same 6 ½ litre of Le Mans; I drove a 4½-litre supercharged Bentley for the first time, and had no success. But the supercharger was approved; it had only just been fitted, and meant an increase of 100h.p. – 35 of which it required for itself – and a far swifter acceleration. To transmit the higher power of a supercharger involves much redesigning of engines, but the difference in speed between "blown" and "unblown" Bentley is a difference between 125 and 108 mph. and more than worth the trouble.

Two rounds of the match between Bentley and Alfa-Romeo had now been fought; the ring for the third round was pitched in Dublin. This course in Phoenix Park is one of the fastest in Europe. It is very short, with a straight of two miles between the Mountjoy and Gough Memorial corners, where some terrible skidding delighted the big crowds, and the remaining two miles curving back again like the round stroke of a capital D. Expectations of furious driving between Mercedes and Bentleys were not to be disappointed.

I did my best to fulfil them myself. Scrap Thistlethwayte was driving his huge white Mercedes, and for the first two hours I sat on its tail, never passing, and rousing the Dublin crowd to an unaccustomed frenzy. Scrap drove brilliantly; he had marked out his course, as an expert, before the race, and adhered to it with an expert's regularity. He drove faster than anyone else, continually lapping at 83 miles an hour, but took no risk nor by reckless cornering endangered the cars behind. This I can attest, as I was so long behind him; but the breakdown, which so often attended Mercedes tried to its limit, made no exception of him. He drew in to refuel, and a lap after, drew in again with 'plug' trouble. So the Mercedes team described it, making light of a far more fundamental evil; but there is a tradition that no car should ever be forced to stop through any fault of its own, and the reason is therefore ascribed to something for which it cannot be blamed. Thus the firm ensures itself against public opinion, for if it took the blame itself, and allowed an honest confession of its failure to be trumpeted by loudspeakers to a crowd of several hundred thousand, how would it ever sell a single car? 'Plug trouble' is a common scapegoat, therefore I was not alarmed when the Mercedes resumed the terrific pace it had previously been setting. Sure enough, a lap or two later, it drew into the pits for the last time. The disagreement was now with a blown gasket, and the only solution withdrawal from the race.

I was now actually in the lead, but on handicap some way behind the Alfa-Romeo driven by

Ivanowsky, and towards the end I saw that his only rival must be Glen Kidston in the 6½-litre 50 h.p. Bentley. Glen had, as always, been driving fast and rather wildly. His skids at Mountjoy Corner are still remembered, and the crowds were waiting only for him. Fifty minutes from the end he had nevertheless made up two of Ivanowsky's three laps handicap. Knowing his recklessness, and aware that I could do nothing myself but try to come in third, I was almost praying that he would pass Ivanowsky. I could see the gap between the two narrowing, both from the track and the agitation of the crowd. There were five laps to go, Glen now only 2½ minutes behind. With four more he had reduced it to a minute, and, as they came into the last lap, only 21 seconds separated them. But it was too much; Glen made a marvellous effort, and caught up all he could, but Ivanowsky crossed the line 14 seconds ahead. So the Italian Alfa ran to earth, like a fox after a great run, only just in time, hounded on by four angry Bentleys in the next four places. Three rounds had been fought to the finish, the first and the second to England, the third to Italy. One more chance of drawing level remained, and the Newtownards circuit was waiting to offer it.

But at the last moment entries were received from all over Europe, and I saw that the opposition would be far stronger than that of a single team. The chief danger was now apprehended from Carraciola's 7-litre supercharged Mercedes, and my 4½-litre Bentley, though supercharged too, stood little chance when we both started from scratch. The Alfas had a handicap of 3 laps, and the baby Austins of five. There were seventy-five entries, and little chance of the race finishing without more than one bad crash. In such a crowd the slightest mistake would be calamitous, not so much for the probability of an accident as for the opening it would give to the cars thronging behind; and that this was realised became from the thousands that streamed into Belfast, expecting a race which only skill could win, and unskill was certain to make sensational. Even the Almighty was inveigled to take an interest, prayers being offered for fine weather in fear of the excitement becoming exaggerated by wet and skiddy roads. But He seemed not to share the general enthusiasm, and morning came with grey skies and an ominous forecast of worse.

A week or two before the race I suggested jokingly to W. O. that he should come as my mechanic instead of Chevrollier, and after decorating the idea with a little merry humour, was about to change the subject, but W. O., who did not seem to have understood the charm of my imagination, suddenly remarked that he rather thought he would come. I was surprised, though I did not resist, and told Bertie Moir, our team manager, who would have nothing to do with it. His disapproval was unmistakable, but only served to confirm our own decision. Then W. O. fell ill, and Bertie Moir grew quite desperate when he found his mind still bent on playing the mechanic. He pleaded on the verge of tears, he used all the obvious weapons of safety and health and team spirit, and, when these did not prevail, produced from his capacious sleeve a trump card. W. O. had forgotten that the insurance policy on his life did not cover motor racing, and when Bertie mentioned that, the smile left his face. He was on the point of surrender, when the insurance agent of the T.T., hearing of his difficulty, came up and promised to insure him in the race for the same sum at a very reasonable figure. Bertie Moir's eloquence could do no more; for three days it had kept W. O. in indecision, and the only trump card had failed. So on the morning of the race W. O. appeared, hardly cured of his illness, in the Bentley overalls with his own name on the pocket, and stepped into the car beside me. He had been practising his job without a pause as often as health and business permitted, so that I never had any qualms about his efficiency. Even had he done nothing, I think my confidence in him would have surmounted all misgivings, a confidence that was more than amply justified.

On the first lap Carraciola led, and a fight began between his Mercedes and Glen Kidston's 6½-litre Bentley. Almost at once the rain began to fall, and soon a storm was sweeping over the course, drenching the drivers and sending up Catherine-wheels of spray from the tyres. Bernard Rubin was the first to crash badly. He skidded, swerved wildly over the road, and, in his own words, overturned slowly but gracefully. He tried to reach the switches to turn off the engine, but the engine had saved him the trouble, and he lay underneath with his mechanic, comfortable enough in body, but expecting another car to run into them any moment. The fear was luckily unfulfilled.

Rain brought no relenting of Carraciola's amazing speed. He continued to pass the grandstand at over 110 mph., the water leaping off the bonnet and spurting in fountains round the wheels, and seemed to find no trouble at all at the corners. Glen stuck to him as bravely, and the crowds settled down under a roof of umbrellas to watch a wonderful race. But at Bradshaw's Brae, going at 90 mph, Glen skidded, could not hold the car, missed a telegraph pole by a miracle and crashed nose first over a ditch.

Not even could this check the Mercedes, which lapped unfailingly at about 70, and then drew in to refill. After 20 laps it gained on the three leading Austins with their handicap of five laps, while Campari lay fourth in an Alfa that started at three laps. My Bentley was running beautifully, and W. O. was delighted. He saw that we had no chance of catching the Mercedes with its three extra litres on level terms, and was as alert throughout the appalling circumstances of the race as any permanent mechanic could have been.

At 25 laps, with only five more to go, one Austin had fallen back, and the lead of the other two been much reduced. Campari was still third and the Mercedes gaining furiously from fourth. The honour of England was in the bonnets of the two infants. As they scuttled past the stands they were greeted with amazed cheers, and whenever Carraciola passed them, they were quite hidden and then seemed to be moving backwards. Another rainstorm swept the road, but only at certain points, so that there was a continual transition from dry to glassy surfaces. At Ballystockart Bridge, Clark, in an O.M., skidded, hit a hedge, and shot back into the opposite bank; his car then stopped, projecting into the middle of the road. Instantly a breakdown gang began to work desperately to move it out of the way, and men ran with flags to signal danger to the cars behind. But they were too late. A Triumph could not stop in time, and the men, caught between this new danger and the wrecked O.M., had no hope of escape. Ambulance crews ran to their aid, but they could do nothing for two of them, and when I passed, there was little but the ruin of two cars and a frightened crowd to attest the tragedy.

Soon after this Carraciola passed Campari, and roared onwards in pursuit of the scurrying Austins. They were passed on the twenty-seventh lap after stopping to refuel, and with three more to go, Campari was 54 seconds in front of Carraciola. Though the English cars were defeated, the crowd could not lose interest in the struggle between the German and Italian. On the twenty-ninth lap, at the beginning of the straight, the white Mercedes flashed past the Alfa, and settled the issue. Campari was second, and the baby Austins had a great welcome as they tripped in third and fourth.

I cannot give enough praise to the inspired driving of the winner; he averaged 72.82 mph, and I, who came in eleventh and second of those who started from scratch, was more than pleased with 69.01. Not for one instant did he falter. The rain was blinding and the roads never more slippery, but whenever he passed me at that terrific speed, I felt no envy, but only incredulity at his skill, his courage and the endurance of his car. He broke records with ease under a deluge of rain, on a road that was at times almost flooded, and never sacrificed the safety of others to his own ambition. To praise his skill is idle now, when the world acknowledges him among its greatest drivers; to commend his modesty would be a less gratuitous tribute. After the cheers and rioting were done, he was asked what had impressed him most during the race. He did not mention the car, nor yet personal enjoyment, with an implied corollary of his own brilliance, but he said he had no words for his admiration of the Austins, and the keenness and information of the younger spectators.

The year ended, as it began, at Brooklands I was driving the supercharged 4½-litre Bentley again, which caught fire and had to retire after 420 miles. The other two Bentleys, driven by Clive Dunfee with Sammy Davis and Jack Barclay with F. C. Clement, had a great race against Kaye Don's Sunbeam. He had entered both the Tiger and the Tigress, which were record-breakers on this track, but they had not been built for long distance, though 20 m.p.h. faster than any other entrant. The Tigress broke a back spring immediately in front of the axle at 120 m.p.h., but was able to reach the pits. After two-thirds of the race, the Tiger was taken over with instructions to drive it as fast as possible. The two Bentleys gave every excuse for obedience, and Jack Barclay had already nearly driven his right-hand front wheel over the top of the banking. For a hundred yards he was unable to right a broadside skid, and as he was going at over 100 mph, can be considered very lucky to have escaped. The tail of the car swung uncontrollably from side to side, but no harm was done. F. C. Clement took over shortly after half-time, and the car ran perfectly to victory. The Tiger was found to have a cracked chassis, and though great caution was needed at the corners, continued at top speed along the straight. John Cobb drove it at an average of 102 mph with a care that more than deserved his third place, and the race was won by the two Bentleys, Jack Barclay's first and Sammy Davis' second, with an Alfa-Romeo fourth.

So the year went out to the fanfare of British superchargers, and hopes were high for the future. Foreign competition was welcome, if it only showed our own superiority. Of course, there had been setbacks, no one was going to belittle Carraciola's performance at Belfast, or Ramponi's at Brooklands, or Ivanowsky's in Phoenix Park, or one or two others that escaped the mind. But there were always the Bentleys, those bulwarks of English complacence;

they would go on next year, and the year after, and several years after that, sweeping the board at Le Mans, wiping their wheels with Brooklands, and, of course, revenging themselves on those sporting foreigners. They would not want any more money, it was common knowledge that they were always years in advance. So reasoned the vague public, and others who should have known better. "Come what may," they cried, "greater speed in the Alfa-Romeos or endurance more assured in the Mercedes, 1930 will see Britain champion of the world."

But all the while the ground was slipping unobtrusively from Britain's feet, and the initiated saw the beginnings of a great cloud coming over the horizon. Where was our English track? Where was the money for an English car to compete with the ceaselessly improving foreign makes? Where were the means of correcting the ignorance and apathy of the public? A period of stagnation seemed to be in the offing, a period of doing one's best and watching other countries better it, as I watched the white Mercedes at Belfast. There might be a miracle, as there had been so many in motor racing before, an epidemic of motormania all over England, teaching the few who went to the races their immense value to industry, and sending to them those who went not, or a fairy godmother turning baby Austins into supercharged Napoleons. If there were no miracle, the motor industry might as well coin a special 1930 medal, and for Britannia on the reverse substitute

Cinderella. Meanwhile the laurels of 1929 were thick enough for a few month's sleep.

They were not the laurels of Brooklands and Le Mans and Ulster alone. At Verneuk Pan, in South Africa, Malcolm Campbell failed to beat Sir Henry Segrave's speed but achieved at the same time a glorious conquest of five-mile and five-kilometre records. To attempt any criticism of him would be an impertinence in me. His determination and his wonderful victories in ultra-high-speed trials are well known and admired from afar, in every country that possesses as much as a mile of straight road.

But as great as Malcolm Campbell, was a man whose name is already as certain of a long, long life as he himself was deprived of it.

It was in 1929 that de Hane Segrave beat the world land record over the measured mile, with a speed of 231 miles an hour. He then promised his wife that he would never race in cars again, and began plans for the speedboat record on Lake Windermere. He asked me if I would come with him and look after one of the engines, to which I agreed at once. Soon afterwards I suggested that he should drive with me at Le Mans, and he promised that he would if I could get his wife's consent. So I went to see her, and after a while persuaded her to release de Hane for that one race. But she gave her permission reluctantly, and I thought she seemed worried. When my preparations for Windermere were finished, and I was about to go up there, I was suddenly taken ill and had to go to bed. De Hane came to say good-bye before his own departure, and told me that, much as he wanted to come with me to Le Mans, his wife was so unhappy about it that he would have to give the idea up. I agreed, and wished him good luck for the record. I went to Le Mans without him and won a comfortable, unadventurous victory. But he was killed on Windermere, as all the world knows, at the moment of the same triumph on the water that he had but lately won on land.

It was a kind fate that took him, not on the sands of a distant country, but in the heart of his own. My own last impression of him was of a man renouncing a great pleasure, not because it was forbidden, but because he thought it might give someone pain. He used to go far out of his way to avoid that, and farther to be of assistance. The greatest of all our drivers, he became great by genius, hard work and complete fairness, and no novice ever asked help or information from him without obtaining it. He was famous for the generosity he showed to others; sincere in his praise of their success, he made light of his own, the quietest and least assuming of men. Until his death he was one of the closest of all my friends. But friendship has led me in no way to exaggerate the light in which he was regarded, by all who knew, or met, or ever heard tell of him.

The 1929 500 Mile event at Brooklands - The Geoffrey Goddard Collection

Birkin and Holder in No. 12 Bentley. JCC Double Twelve Race. Brooklands 1929 - Courtesy Brooklands Motor Museum

Birkin on his way to first Le Mans win in Bentley Speed 6, winner 1929 Le Mans - National Motor Museum, Beaulieu

Victory at Le Mans in the Bentley Speed 6 with Wolf Barnato. 16th June 1929 - The Geoffrey Goddard Collection

Birkin and W.O. Bentley at the 1929 TT - The Geoffrey Goddard Collection

The 1929 Irish GP Eirann Cup in which Birkin finished 3rd. 13th July 1929 - The Geoffrey Goddard Collection

Birkin with Dorothy Paget who saved the team from a premature demise. 18th July 1930 - PA Images/Alamy Stock Photo

Preparation for 1930 Brooklands Whit Monday event - Courtesy Brooklands Motor Museum

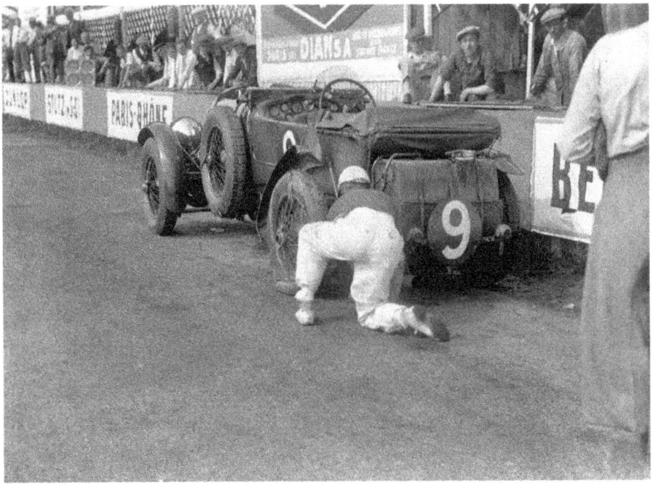

1930 Le Mans. Birkin working on a flat tyre of his Bentley Blower no. 9 co-driven with Jean Chassagne - The Geoffrey Goddard Collection

Birkin racing at the 1930 Irish GP Eirann Cup. 19th July 1930 - The Geoffrey Goddard Collection

— CHAPTER VIII —

The Wearing of the Green

At the beginning of the new year it was announced that a fairy godmother in the earthly guise of the Hon. Dorothy Paget had come to the Cinderella of British motor industry. She bought in March my three Bentleys, among them the track single-seater which was begun at the end of 1929, and increased them to four. Hers was a most sporting action, prompted by a genuine sympathy with a cause in which she herself was well-versed. It gave a new lease of life to the motor-racing world in England, and indeed it seems to be women who have, and use generously, the disposal of that lease. The cars were, of course, her property, but I was to run them for her under the famous green colours.

The Brooklands season opened with the usual camaraderie and back-slapping, and a new bait for the public – the 'Mountain' course, which had twenty hairpins and was twelve miles long with the whole lap in view of the spectators. This race was won by Lord Howe. A malignant rumour spread at the meeting that

Kaye Don had been killed on Daytona sands in his attempt on the land speed record. Sir Henry Segrave telephoned from Paris for confirmation, and much distress was caused. I do not share the view that such stories are inevitable; they should never be allowed to germinate, especially concerning a subject so wrapped in little superstitions as motor racing, until there is no possible doubt of their accuracy on every point.

Kaye Don then held the lap record for Brooklands with a figure of 134.2 mph, which I was determined to defeat. So I arranged a match with Jack Dunfee in which he was to drive a Sunbeam and I the 4½-litre supercharged single-seater. At the last moment Jack had trouble with a connecting rod, and I raced alone. But I did not reach the course until an hour before the start. I was in Le Touquet with Babe Barnato, where he bet me a dinner at the Casino that I would not break the record. I flew to Brooklands, where there was a large crowd, and took the car round once to warm it up. After that I tried never to lift my foot from the accelerator; over the bumpy surface, I was once in the air for 40 feet and the car too, but it did two laps of 134.6 and 135.3, and so set up a new record. The car running so beautifully that in a later race it did two more laps of 135, and the day was epitomised in a letter I received afterwards, extolling "the phenomenal way the car settled down on the track, literally twice as steady as 90 per cent, of the others at 100 mph." I flew back to Le Touquet in the evening and had my dinner with Babe.

On May 9th and 10th the second Double 12 race was held, and a fine British victory spoilt by a terrible tragedy. Two Bentleys, a Riley and an Aston Martin led an Alfa-Romeo in the first four places, and Babe and Clement drove the winning Bentley. Not one of the first four was supercharged, and the triumph was so great that optimism for the industry began to return. I retired at 4.30 on Friday, and at that time the debutante Talbots were achieving easily the most remarkable success. At about 7 o'clock, one of them, No. 21, was just ahead of its fellow, 22, and tried to pass an Alfa in front, but found a slower car in its way. It swerved, and its off rear wheel locked with the near front wheel of the 22 Talbot behind. It rushed on into a telegraph post and overturned without hurt to its occupants; but the other, dragged helplessly nearer the edge, crashed over the spiked railings on to the crowd. The mechanic was killed at once, and the driver, Rahagliati, badly hurt; a man was caught underneath the car and killed, and ten people were injured. The third Talbot was at once withdrawn.

On June 9th Kaye Don equalled and broke my record in two races. His former record of 134.2 had been made with his Sunbeam, the Tiger, and the new one of 137.58 was with its mate, the Tigress, proof positive that the female of the species is more deadly than the male. We had never met level in a race, and I was resolved to make another attempt to hold the record.

The crowds at Brooklands were beginning to increase, and it seemed as if the public was at last beginning to awake from its indifference to motor racing. But Brooklands was not the Mecca of the sport; English successes there did not carry a quarter the weight of successes on the great tracks in Ireland and the Continent.

On June 13th there was a Motor-Car Rally at Maidenhead, which was extremely popular. Babe and I were among the judges. Perhaps more foreigners were attracted to that than to any other motoring event in England; perhaps we can go on attracting them by such entrancing Concours d'Elegance and intriguing obstacle races, and so never need to build a first-class road circuit. Think of the economy! And of course it need not always be at Maidenhead - Blackpool would welcome it, or Weston-super-Mare. How could people suggest that there was anything wrong with the motor industry!

The first fortnight of June passed, and the words 'Le Mans' crept into the motor columns once more, but for many weeks they had been in my own mind, coupled, like Calais with Philip on Mary Tudor's heart, a place with a name, Le Mans with Carraciola. I knew that he was certain to renew our last year's rivalry, and, though no longer a member of the official team, I was as eager to meet him. His opposition was now, in all races, of much more concern to me than the Alfa-Romeos, who had at one time been my chief anxiety. Moreover, another Bentley victory at Le Mans would complete the hat-trick, after which I suppose we could keep the course. I had been ill for some time, but decided that the best way to forget one feeling was to acquire another more violent, and pined for an exceptionally nerve-racking race. On Monday or Tuesday of practice, the spare car ran its big ends, and on the fourth night threw its fly-wheel off. The mechanics were busy day and night; seven or eight of them worked in the car, and if any of these once left his place, it was filled instantly by another in waiting. We then discovered that incorrect setting of the headlamps, and the petrol supplied by the club were causing dangerous overheating; either 70/30 per cent Benzol or pure Benzol had to be used, no intermediary proportion was permitted. So on the Thursday I had a conference with W. O., and we made up our minds to run his and Dorothy Paget's teams together, leagued against the Mercedes. We knew that it was faster than us, over 125 mph to 115, and that its acceleration was also superior. So we thought it best to run the S.C. cars on pure Benzol and increase the compression ratio, which would give us a little more speed than the Mercedes, but stress our engine more than I wanted. The mechanics had worked indefatigably since their arrival, and were exhausted; between Wednesday and Sunday night they had only ten hours' sleep. They could not set the lamps and alter the compression in time, so only two of the supercharged cars were treated.

It was obvious to both of us that a car must be detailed to wear down the Mercedes, make it use its supercharger – which is engaged by a clutch – and so overstrain its engine and put it out of the race. Otherwise it might cling throughout all hut the closing laps on the leading Bentley's tail, conserving its strength to shoot suddenly ahead at the end and win.

The policy of wearing down was one after my own heart, and I promised to exploit it with all my ability, on one condition exacted as a *quid pro quo* for Dorothy Paget. I made W.O. agree not to race the second supercharged Bentley with the official team, if at the end of the race either of the others had a chance of victory. My own hopes were dashed continually by tyre trouble: there was a tropical heat, and I think the rubber was too thick, so that centrifugal force flung it away from the canvas and caused it to split. Tyres on racing cars are always of the thinnest rubber available.

The three official Bentleys were told to give me every opening for a clear run, and, as I started at the back and they in the front with the Mercedes first of all, it was a command to be obeyed. I saw a glorious race ahead of me; my path was to be cleared, my car and my own strength strained to their limits, and with luck the great Mercedes would break up. There were only seventeen of us, and we looked very forlorn between the huge crowds.

The Mercedes was first away, with the sun shining like silver on its bonnet, and after Pontlieue I began to creep up to it. Glen Kidston was on its tail in No. 4, and after the S-bend at Arnage let me pass in obedience to instructions. There was now no one between me and Carraciola. The other Bentleys had given way, and the rest of the field were also left. I came past the grandstand with Glen a little way behind, and a cloud of dust some way in front pointing the Mercedes. It finished the second lap at an average of 86 m.p.h., but I caught up a second or two and on the third lap averaged 88. I could see the car more clearly now through the dust. Glen had fallen behind, and as I passed the pits, I saw huge blackboards thrust over the Mercedes counter. The Germans were changing their tactics, but there was no slackening of Carraciola's pace, and I supposed the signals were for greater speed. Our plan was succeeding.

On the third lap I decided to wait for the straight before Mulsanne and there pass him. We roared down the hill towards it, and took the bend and came into the three kilometres of clear road. I heard the supercharger wailing as I approached, and when still 100 yards away, another stranger sound from my own car. There was a flap and then a hang, as if I had run over a tin can, and when I looked out I saw a crumpled mudguard. Pictures rose before me of 1928 and the Bentley derelict by the roadside; but in a second or two I was level with the Mercedes and travelling at over 125 mph. Carraciola never suspected that I could have been so near; the whinings of his supercharger stopped him hearing any other car behind, and he was only just settling into his stride, driving a little in the middle of the road. I saw there was the barest margin to squeeze through. Mulsanne was coming nearer, and so I took my chance, and risking the damage to the tyre, passed the Mercedes with two wheels on the grass. The car rocked, but got by just in time for me to change down and go round the corner. Carraciola said that this was one of the greatest shocks of his life, to see a car, whose imminence he had not dreamt of, come tearing past him at that speed on the outmost edge of the road, with a bare patch in its left rear tyre. I did not know myself that I had thrown the complete tread, and though I saw agitation in the pits and heard cries from the spectators, I could not afford to slacken speed with the Mercedes wailing behind. We passed Mulsanne once more; and as the Bentley raced out of the Arnage bend, it lurched and got into a wild skid. I knew only then that the tyre had gone; it was torn to shreds, and, as I hobbled into the pits at under 40, the Mercedes passed me.

It had been a thrilling interlude, of the kind dear to my heart, combining a competition between two wonderful cars with a policy devised for the benefit of a team, and once I had changed my tyre I set out on the chase refreshed. It had been taken up by Sammy Davis in No. 3, who had passed Glen Kidston in No. 4 at the command of the team manager, and now kept second place for thirteen laps, or over 130 miles. I was lying seventh, and whenever Carraciola came near me, or I near him, I saw him endeavouring to lower his speed, and always being hustled on by the ubiquitous Bentleys. Again I had tyre trouble, and lost 3 minutes changing a wheel, but I managed to creep up into sixth place behind the Bentleys and Brisson's Stutz. It was a fighting race; dark had not yet fallen, and I had already had more adventures than usual in the whole 24 hours. I was not out of the running yet.

Carraciola still led, striving most gallantly against a pack of relentness Furies. When I failed, Sammy Davis dogged him, and at 9.30 Babe Barnato took Sammy's place. Not for one second could the Mercedes relax, and I felt that soon, surely, it must crack. Chassagne had now taken over my Bentley, and Clive Dunfee Sammy Davis; but I watched from the pits for Clive in vain. Carraciola came round, and handed over to Christian Werner; the German pit work was not expert, and much of the lead on No. 4 was here lost. Werner had not Carraciola's pace, and when Babe brought No. 4 back on his first lap, I knew from its running and my experience of Babe, that the Mercedes would not stay long in front. Dr. Benjafield followed in No. 8, and at last the news came of Clive Dunfee, who had skidded at Pontlieue and was now endeavouring to dig the Bentley out of the sand. He worked courageously for a long while, and finally came back exhausted; but not so Sammy Davis, who went off with one eye sightless from a stone flung up by the Mercedes, that had splintered the glass of his goggles. For another hour he scooped the sand away with the spare headlamp glass, and at last found the front axle and wheels bent beyond all hope.

My Bentley now lay seventh, behind the two Stutz, and night was approaching. All the old lights, that two years of Le Mans had taught me to recognise and await, began to come out; in the pits the shaded lamps glared inwards, and coloured lanterns hung round the dancing places. The air was cool to those not racing, and few attempted to sleep; in the car parks crowds of private cars still lay huddled together like shadows, until one would swing out and join the river of lights back to the town. But, whatever the weather, there would have been many to watch the great struggle between Mercedes and Bentley. A Stutz caught fire and blazed like a beacon by the side of the track; the glare was blinding as we passed it, and the margin of road so small that we drove through almost a wall of flames. The fading glow lit up the tall trees, throwing the figures of the crowd around into silhouette, and for hours the dark smoke drifted like a ghost across the road. But on raced the Bentley, now just in front of Werner and the Mercedes. Carraciola took over, and passed a few yards beyond the burning Stutz; but at 9.30 Babe regained his lead and kept it till 11.20. For half an hour Carraciola led and for the few minutes before midnight Babe once more. Midnight had scarcely finished striking when the Mercedes passed again, but could not hold its position for over 2 laps. Babe put in to refuel, and a second or two after, Carraciola drew in past him with oil trouble. For 2 minutes the cars were motionless, separated by a few yards, while their drivers ran to and from the pits; groups of officials stood round and the pit lights shone on the white Mercedes. The Bentley was away first, but Carraciola caught up before it was clear of the pits. I had lost much of my own enthusiasm, and felt tired after illness and the exhausting early stages. But at 1.30 I saw the Bentley was leading, and in an hour's time the Mercedes returned to the pits. At first its headlights shone brilliantly ahead, then flickered and finally went out. The second battery was exhausted, and the engine would not start nor the lights work. So Carraciola admitted defeat, with no shame to driver or car. They had fun alone for 10 hours, and held more than its own against a meticulously prepared team of five Bentleys; to have lasted as long as that was miraculous. I retired after 20 hours with a broken connecting rod.

The race went on, of course, and the Bentleys did their hat-trick. It was also Babe's third consecutive victory, and he and Glen were almost invisible under the bouquets. The cheering died down, and as thoughts of sleep began to revolve in the head, and the crowds melted away, a small voice piped up and, "Now," it said, "now we must all get ready for Dublin."

So in a month's time, in the middle of July, to Dublin we all went. But in that month great changes had taken place; the Bentleys had withdrawn their official team, and two more Mercedes had appeared to reinforce Carraciola. One was to be driven by

Malcolm Campbell, and the other by Francis Howe; but neither of them, though tremendously fast both, could compete with Carraciola's short-chassis model, which was capable of speeds not yet attained in road racing. It was silver and white, and the other two blue and white. There would be no mercy, least of all in Phoenix Park. Elaborate improvements had been made in the stands and a huge crowd was awaited; tunnels ran under the course, and the start on Saturday was timed for 2.30 instead of 1.30, for the benefit of the working people. Very early in the week the thrills began. On Tuesday Malcolm Campbell made the lap record of 87.7 m.p.h., exceeding the previous year's by over 4 m.p.h. On Wednesday he beat it with 88.7, and an hour or two afterwards Carraciola equalled this in the rain. On Thursday Malcolm Campbell did 89.7. The pace was becoming frightening. But Malcolm said that he would have to go faster than this to wipe off the handicaps. We had had trouble with the other two "blown," or supercharged Bentleys, and I saw to my horror that on mine rested the responsibility of defeating the Mercedes. The others, Alfa-Romeos, Talbots, Austins all paled in my eyes before the Mercedes, I could think of nothing but my next round with Carraciola. The Le Mans tables were turned, it was for the "blown" Bentleys to carry the green alone against the white and silver and blue. I had my handicap of two laps, everything was perfectly fair. There remained our third round; and after that whatever happened would be compared with Ulster and Le Mans, and Bentley and Mercedes lie in the balances. Bitterly as I may have been disappointed about our other Bentleys, I know that, from a personal point of view, I would not have changed the conditions for the world.

The weather was fine at the start, but a threat of rain hung in the air, which I prayed might not be fulfilled. Carraciola in the rain has no equal. The nineteen cars got away remarkably quickly, in 5 seconds there was not one left for the crowds' amusement. At Mountjoy corner I was in front of all save Carraciola and Francis Howe, and on the back stretch of all save Carraciola. He passed the stands 5 seconds in front of me, and it was clear that he commanded much of the popular sympathy. We raced by a little S.A.R.A. that had been left behind, and from that moment the crowd had no peace. Almost every three minutes for the next two hours we came round with the gap widening between, until the cloud of the Mercedes' dust began to vanish ahead of me and my two laps handicap to dwindle. Other cars came after us, to be quickly caught up and passed by a lap or more; but so far I felt that there was no race save the race between Mercedes and Bentley, and that it was for this the crowd stood straining their eyes. I had heard the Mercedes' supercharger cutting in and out, and knew it had a reserve of speed still in hand. As I came by the stand on the second lap, the loudspeaker was braying inaudibly, and there followed a tumult of applause. Carraciola had beaten the lap record at 90.8 miles an hour; on the third lap he passed a Sunbeam. The sky was overcast with gray clouds, and a little before three the rain came down. It fell in torrents, streaming across the bonnet of the car and blurring the road in front, making the roads like ice and the corners a death-trap to the reckless. It brought out an army of umbrellas and sent those who had none scurrying for shelter; it put an entirely new face on the course, but it could not change the speed of the Mercedes. Carraciola was in his element, and I wish I could have watched him closer, as he flew down the back stretch at 130 and braked along that treacherous surface to slow for the Gough corner; his skill and confidence were beyond comparison. He was now leading me by 63 seconds, gradually wearing down my handicap, which was equal to about five and a half minutes. Approaching the Zoo I was some way behind, but not too far to see the Mercedes through the blur of rain skid across the road, and turn round twice as it tried to slow down for the corner; it seemed impossible to stop overturning, but as I came nearer, somehow or other Carraciola steadied it, ended the skid straight, and shot off again to wild applause. But that mistake brought his lead down to 48 seconds, and behind me Malcolm Campbell was coming up in his blue and silver car. He had a terrible skid which nearly flung his car off the course, but continued to overtake me. For a little while my race was with him, but shortly after passing he drew into the pits, and there lost over two laps. I passed him as the floorboards of his car were being lifted and Pyrene squirted over the clutch. It was bad luck that he should have had trouble at such a triumphant moment.

I was still holding Carraciola on handicap, but every lap a few seconds increased his lead; on one he gained fourteen, but on the next only three. Campari in the Alfa slipped into third place, and gave an exhibition of wild Italian cornering; but we were alone in the lead, and one of my laps slipping helplessly away. In front of the grandstand a dog strolled on to the course, and I swerved to avoid it. The time was now past four. It seemed a long while since I had seen the Mercedes, but as I came into the straight I heard the moaning of its supercharger behind. I put my foot down for all I was worth; but it was of no avail. We raced towards the grandstand; I saw the white bonnet with its silver star, and then Carraciola himself, staring ahead in his white peaked cap, so close in the Mercedes' left-hand drive that I could almost have touched him. For a second or two we were level, and then he was past, heading for Mountjoy corner, his spray flying up round my eyes. There were 24 of the 60 laps to go, and I calculated that I would just hold him on the very last of all. He drew into the pits to refuel and there I passed him, but he was away in 69 seconds. A lap later I had to draw in myself, and as I hurled in the cans of petrol, the Mercedes flashed by again. The crowds, whose excitement kept them on their feet waving and shouting as we passed, cheered me as I got away after 65 seconds. I had gained four on him, and for the next five laps I held him. There was half an hour more before the end, and about two-thirds of a laps' handicap left; I thought I could just get home before he caught me. But a little wisp of smoke came floating through the bonnet, and then another the other side, and another, until a grey cloud had risen in front of me; oil began to spout on to my legs, the heat was too great, and I had to stop at the pits. An oil pipe – every Bentley had a duplicate strapped on – was changed in what seemed an hour; 2 minutes 48 seconds were lost, and as I jumped in and rushed off again, the Mercedes was approaching. It was 7⅖ seconds behind, and at Mountjoy corner it caught me. I could hold it no longer, and with more smoke from the bonnet filtering into my eyes I was passed. With six more laps to go, I stopped again, to find the oil blown on to the hot exhaust, and the Mercedes raced by with another lap's lead. As it disappeared past the stands to Mountjoy, and as I struggled desperately with the oil, I heard the loudspeakers croaking triumphantly, that the 7-litre Mercedes Benz, driven by Rudolf Carraciola, had just completed a record lap at 91.3 miles an hour. Victory was assured.

But worse was waiting for me. I dropped to third behind Campari, stopped again and lost a close race with Francis Howe for a place. As I came round on my final laps, I heard the frantic cheering for Carraciola, and came in at last to find him smiling and dirty and shy, hung with garlands of flowers, trying to escape from the crowds with his Frau, who had timed him all the way and was in ecstasies.

I cannot wish for a better race, nor a finer opponent. I thought in 1929 that he could never improve on his performance in the rain at Belfast, but to-day he had proved me wrong.

From that hour until this, neither my mechanic Whitlock nor myself have been able to account for the failure of the other two Bentleys. After 5 laps they suddenly lost oil pressure, while my own car continued without trouble till the last half-hour. No pressure was registered, a fault usually caused by a broken oil pipe or failure of the pump to work and circulate the oil. But everything seemed in order, and the thing remains a mystery. The oil pressure in my own car did not drop enough to hinder, but it was oil that caused my collapse.

So directly the cars were back in the works, we sat down to consider the problem of lubrication. The T.T. race was due in a month, and when the time came to ship the cars to Ulster, we thought we had the solution. To have trusted to luck would have been ridiculous on any occasion, but at that particular moment criminal. It was my last chance in 1930 to draw level with Carraciola; he had won at Belfast in 1929, and a month ago in Phoenix Park, but he had failed at Le Mans. Either the scales were to balance over this last struggle at Belfast, or the German would hopelessly outweigh the British. The day of reckoning had come; there could be no postponing of settlement till 1931, for who knew that 1931 would see him still racing the same cars, or even racing at all? And there was a far deeper issue than mere friendly competition between two drivers; the prestige of England was involved in it. Already Miss Paget had hinted that she would not extend her patronage to a second season. For a year she had played the fairy godmother with patriotism and generosity, and that year was shortly to be revealed as a seven days' wonder. At the end of 1929 motor experts had prayed for a miracle, and behold! Dorothy Paget. She had thrown the lifebelt to the sinking sport, and for a few more strokes it had kept its head above water. But when the lifebelt was withdrawn, what could stop it drowning under the risen floods of foreign competition?

Success in the Ulster race might attract real aid, failure could elicit nothing but sympathy, and Carraciola, for all his charm, was unlikely to lose out of kindness. There were other dangers as formidable, but less familiar than he. The Alfa-Romeo team was to be led by the greatest driver in the world, Tazio Nuvolari, assisted by Varzi, Campari, Minoia and Ramponi. They were all very fine drivers, and one or two of them notoriously wild, capable of racing desperately against each other and breaking up their team. Only the very greatest of team managers could have controlled them, and only the very greatest of team managers did. His name was Giovannini; his position was that of an impresario producing an opera in which all the leading roles are taken by temperamental stars. Yet he contrived to satisfy everyone and calm every storm. He had a deep insight into the qualities of men and of cars; he speaks Italian, French, German, Spanish and English, and needs them all. He possesses the most delightful sense of humour; and that also he needs. But in this event much of his work was done for him by a telegram from Mussolini. It was read to the Italian team and ran thus: "I am sure that in a strange land each of you will battle only for a victory for the Italian flag, forgetting all jealousy and personal feuds." When they heard these noble words, which sound as if they came straight from the Anthology, the Italian drivers, like naughty schoolboys, gripped each others' hands and swore to be good.

All these influences roused the racers, and even many of the spectators, to a pitch of nervous agitation. The village of Comber, when accused of apathy, flamed into indignant protest. In practice Carraciola covered the 14-mile circuit in 10 minutes 54 seconds, and I in 10 minutes 57 seconds. A few nights before the race he was coming to dine with me and the rest of the Bentleys' team, when his car skidded, and he arrived late in a taxicab. He was much chaffed about this, and told that it was such a bad omen, he had better withdraw his Mercedes at once. He was as excited as I was, though he had fewer interests involved. On the eve of the race his name began to be coupled with a rumour of an unexpected discovery by the scrutineers; little groups collected to discuss it, and the stewards sat long in conclave. No one was quite sure what had happened, until an official announcement came that Carraciola had been disqualified. The supercharger of his car had been found to be 3 millimetres longer than standard. Malcolm Campbell, who entered the car, was not aware of it, and Carraciola had no idea that it infringed a rule. It was actually he who had pointed it out, comparing it with the standard superchargers on the other two Mercedes. He was given leave to change it if he wished, and as he had time to do by making his mechanics work all night. But he refused; and so in the morning I went on to the course and saw that the silver and white angel of victory was not there. Every one deeply regretted its absence, and to me the race seemed suddenly to have lost much of its thrill. But a little before the start Carraciola and his wife came down in the car to watch, and the Irish crowd, always sympathetic to the smallest misfortune, cheered him as if he had just won. When I went up to tell him how sorry I was, he attempted to make light of it; but I could see that he was bitterly disappointed, and his wife was almost in tears.

The race was a very good one, and also about as bad as it could be. The Alfa-Romeos were first, second, and third, driven by Nuvolari – who thus became champion of Italy – Campari and Varzi, and so wiped off the Bentley conquest of Le Mans. All finished at an average of over 80. I was leading in the first lap and Bertie Moir was close behind in another of the green Bentleys he was driving instead of Beris Wood, who was ill, and had not raced since 1925. He put up a great fight at Le Mans that year, passing de Hane Segrave after a long struggle but later being forced to retire. He was then at the height of his fame, much of which was earned in hill climbing, and retired to walk to the altar instead. He is the most genial of men, with a deep laugh starting in a gurgle and slowly swelling to a crescendo that makes everyone else laugh too; and he is an expert at pouring oil on troubled waters. There was one occasion when a car refused to start, and no one could find what was the matter with it, until suddenly Bertie Moir shouted, "Hit the accumulator-box with a hammer!" Someone hit it, and the self-starter then worked without a murmur.

Early in the race Nuvolari and Campari passed me, the latter leading; notices were put out to warn him of his driving, but at first he seemed to ignore them. I then saw him, some distance out from the pits, going at about 10 m.p.h., shouting in his famous operatic voice at a great regiment of officials shouting back, waving blackboards and tumbling over each other to catch him up. Then he rushed off, and as I came past at about 100 , I nearly blew Giovannini back into the pits.

At 1 p.m. my Bentley made a record of 76.2 mph for its class, and Kaye Don of 72.8 for his. Our successes both ended in a crash, from which we were very lucky to escape. The mechanic jumped out, but

Don was only just rescued in time. I fell back to sixth, and at one time missed a photographer by less than inches, as we raced down the narrow Comber street; the Bentley skidded as he was poising his camera, and changing his mind quicker than any one I have ever seen, he leapt into a doorway. As we approached Ballystockart Bridge, where there is a lefthand bend, my mechanic Whitlock began to look at the floorboards as if something had broken, and I said, "What's happened?" The course was very slippery, and I found I was in the wrong position on the first bend for the bend that followed. This is one so the worst mistakes that can be made, and I had to wrench the steering wheel; there was a slight front wheel skid, and my left front hub struck a telegraph pole at 90. The tail swung round, we went into an opposite skid, and began a series of gyrations on three wheels. There seemed no chance of not dashing straight into a crowd of people who stood unprotected by the roadside; but with what remained of the steering I managed, God knows how, to avoid them, and the car went gracefully into a stone wall at about 60, knocked it down, turned round and went into it again head on. Never at any instant was there a suggestion of the car overturning, neither my mechanic nor I felt any alarm for ourselves; nor, when we ran into the wall was there the very least shock. The car was *hors de combat;* and when we walked away, the crowd cheered, as indeed I should have cheered if I had missed death by as little as some of them missed it.

The last months of that year were a little sad, for the end of the great Bentley combination was in sight. There has been a time when separately managed Bentleys ran with the official team, but since the latter's withdrawal one foot had been literally in the grave, and now the other was following. With it was vanishing the prestige of England, which that one firm had faithfully upheld. I question if we shall ever see again as cheery a crowd as the so-called "Bentley Boys" - Glen Kidston, Babe Barnato, Scrap Thistlethwayte, Sammy Davis, Bernard Rubin, Beris Wood, Jack and poor Clive Dunfee and myself. We were always seen together; we had the same manner of speech, the same jokes among ourselves. Jack Dunfee was our official jester; it was he who invented the "School." W.O. was its headmaster; a car was a satchel, and petrol was ink; Jack Dunfee turned every incident into something to do with the "School," and talked about it in an appalling drawl. All this may seem childish to those who cannot see how precious was that spirit of gaiety, when we went together to Le Mans or Belfast, or wherever it might be, to pit the green Bentleys against the foreigners. But a few, who can imagine the common interests and diversity of character in our team, the friendships formed with other teams, the endless discussions and the dinner parties, will understand how changed the time seemed when all of it was past.

I had another race this year, the Gold Star Handicap at Brooklands; I drove a Bugatti and won but was disqualified, and rightly, for crossing the line. This has been made the subject of so much controversy, of which there is sufficient in the next chapter, that I have not discussed it at length.

— INTERIM —

England, My England

I have at last reached the subject which is the kernel of the book, the present lethargy of the English motor industry. I have tried to arrange my material, like a revue, with a sequence of light sketches preparing for a moment of seriousness. All the former pages were a prelude to this; the thrills and descriptions, however inadequate, were meant to prepare the ground for the seeds of instruction and probably fruitless criticism. So do not skip this chapter without a determined effort to read it; otherwise you will be unable to boast that you "managed to wade through the book."

I have not minced my words, nor veiled my true opinions in a cloak of polite suggestion; innuendo is not my forte, and the subject has a nature far too urgent for coy understatement. I have condemned much that has been for long accepted as satisfactory, paid little respect to merit that is purely traditional, and run down my own country. But if any one points to me, as true to the type that sneers about things in which it has had its little success, he is making an unfair judgment. I express my subsequent views with regret; they give me no malicious pleasure, I am not chuckling to think of some people's faces as they read them. Others have held them, with a longer experience than mine, and kept them as it were in an envelope, expecting them to be aired publicly in the normal course of events. But events did not take their normal course. Those who should have acted have been too afraid or too ignorant; and the time is come to break our private seal. I happened to have been asked for a book; and as a book is a better medium of publicity than a few stray articles, I have become the spokesman of many who own a better right. If my sincerity is in question, proof will follow to attest it. If my facts are doubted, I am willing, should it give any one any satisfaction, to stake my reputation on their accuracy.

The purpose of speed is as popular a matter for debate as the use of climbing Mount Everest or the advantages of a classical education. There is a set of stereotyped arguments for either side, which may be borrowed from any schoolmaster. The opinion of the public does not vary, whatever advance the subject may have made, and however pressing its need for recognition. The public regard motor racing as an instrument for thrilling the driver at first hand, and themselves at second. They give it an aloof patronage in the abstract, and an enthusiastic submission in the flesh. But its devotees would always be put in a cigarette-picture series of Kings of Speed, rather than of Benefactors to Civilisation.

Let me explain that I am about to refer to the genuine Grand Prix type of racing car. This is a pure racing machine, built for that one purpose in Continental Grand Prix road races. It is opposite to the Bentley and other English cars, which have competed in the races for standard models bearing a close resemblance to those used by the general public, and in races of the Ulster T.T. and the Le Mans type.

The misapprehension is due to ignorance, and not obtuseness. It is not understood that the object of motor racing, as Lord Howe said in his Foreword, is to develop the breed. Yet every improvement or experiment in the last many years has been tested and valued in a race; front-wheel brakes, shock-absorbers, superchargers, efficient engines, efficient dynamos, lamps, steering, mudguards, windscreens, tyres – all of these have been developed through failure and success on road and track to the stage which they have now reached. The reliability of an ordinary touring car, such as you may possess yourself, has only been achieved through racing and only can be so achieved. I have heard people say that such-and-such a make won because it was faster than any other. This is fiddlesticks. A tremendously high standard of endurance, efficiency in build, and preparation of springs, gears, steering, lights and engine are essential before a car is so much as in the running for victory. A great race like Le Mans taxes every part to the utmost for 24 hours; it demands even more from a car than does a young undergraduate with a penchant for speed. It is not surprising that a nation's motor trade derives more impetus and publicity and financial profit from winning such an event than the most elaborate advertising campaign could ever give it. International prestige is of the greatest moment to the industry; and any country that does not exert its last breath to uphold its own, is guilty of unpardonable stupidity. We have committed that crime. No real attempt has been made in England to inculcate the all-importance of motor racing into the mind of the public, and when there is no public to arouse it, the idleness of manufacturers turns to stagnation. It is not so on the Continent; either the government has emphasised or the people themselves have been alive to the significance of their races; they have attended them unfailingly, and thereby aided them financially and guaranteed their continuity. But their enthusiasm has been appreciative, not merely excited by speed and the hope of accident. They know they are watching a spectacle, in which their country's reputation and part of its prosperity are at stake.

The attitude of the English crowds, owing to this ignorance, cannot fail, to the really interested mind, to be a contemptible one. But they are not to blame for it, for no chance to acquire the necessary information has ever come their way. The acid test of a car is a road-course. Throughout the length and breadth of England there is no road-course. Thank God! sigh the beauty-lovers, the anti-litter societies, the institutions for the Preservation of Rural Spots, and whenever the word speed is murmured, they rush up on to a high and lonely hill in their little shorts and open shirts, and setting their enormous banner in the ground, cry, "No roadster shall pass this way!" But it is silly to assume that a road-course must spoil a lovely view. The Nürburg Ring has spoilt nothing, the noise does not make lunatics of its neighbours. They are proud of it, as the people of Stratford are proud of Shakespeare; and the white road cuts through the monotony of the landscape, and enlivens it, as the race-course at Goodwood. But if the objectors are adamant, there are plenty of hideous districts to be made more hideous, or more attractive, by the erection of a road-course. It is an infinitesimal difficulty, but I shall return to it. It has deterred no country on the Continent, and I am ashamed to have to draw the comparison. Each nation has its own magnificent course. There is usually racing every week-end on one or other from April till the end of September, attended always by a great crowd. Some nations, combining utility with pleasure, have made motor racing their national sport. The continental Press devotes much space to it, and lack of intelligence in the spectators would be inexcusable. No wonder that foreign makes head the market, when their progress is continually being promoted, so far from being neglected or even impeded. No wonder that Englishmen with a proper desire for the good car turn reluctantly to Alfa-Romeo, Bugatti and Mercedes. Until 1930 the Bentleys were as good and sometimes better than any of these makes; but they could not thrive on nothing, and continue to dance the public's tune when no one paid the piper. *Go and win at Le Mans!* we were told; and we won at Le Mans again and again. *Go and win in Ireland!* and there, too, we did not disgrace ourselves, nor yet at Boulogne nor yet at Pau, nor yet at Nürburg.

But in 1930 our resources came to an end. The backing of the country was indispensable, and for that the country must be able to take an interest, and for that a road-course was the only solution. Men whose names were well known in racing used all their influence and exhausted all their energy to enable its erection, before the next season opened and found England bare of car, course or means to obtain either. Lord Howe devised a scheme for a course in Richmond Park. But Richmond Park was only a suggestion, to set a controversy alight and kindle popular interest, and there were many others. Yet however eloquently their case was pleaded, and however vehemently the need was emphasised, all the plans, expense and labour beat themselves in vain against one tiny little omnipotent Statute. I have not the legal phrasing of it, but its effect was this, that no public highway should at any time be closed for the purpose of speed trials. It is easy to repeal, or revoke, or dip in whatever Parliamentary Lethe is used for foolish laws; but it still exists.

I know, and everybody else knows, and it is regrettable, that the English are quick to observe small troubles, but slow to consider the great; they like to sit down and consider them in comfort, while the bad influence spreads and spreads until it has become a shame and a reproach. For more than a year, leaders of the motor-racing world have been trying to convince enough people to make the removal of that Statute worthwhile; but we are still afraid of finding one day that it has gone, and left us no nearer getting our course. The public must show unmistakably that it is behind the venture, that it would take the chances accompanying success to learn a little about its importance and show itself at heart as patriotic as any foreigner. It is very little to ask from a people that has always vaunted its patriotism, and what more pleasant way of proving it than by cheering the green cars again to victory, and watching the prestige of England roar safely past under the bonnet of her own racing cars?

It enrages me beyond words to hear Lord Howe and Sir Malcolm Campbell and myself and others, who have done our utmost to help our motor industry against the odds, pilloried for taking the only alternative of driving foreign cars, by men who have never lifted a finger. Would they rather we took to shuttlecock, and let British names disappear from the list of drivers as well as of cars? These bogus patriots are, no doubt, already accusing me of having an axe to grind – that have done so before – and declaring that I only make a fuss because I want a car to drive. So I do want a car; the question is not of its existence, but of its nationality.

But I cannot see whence an English car, which must be built, of course, for the road, is going to appear. The English manufacturers, of whom a little might justly be expected, have chosen to exploit a policy or pose of aloof magnificence which is without any kind of pretext. They have shut themselves up in a high tower, like the Lady of Shalott, deliberately excluding the real view and preferring a blurred, jaundiced outlook on what is happening in their own world. Their isolation is self-imposed; it is selfish already, and continuing will become disastrous. I can see no very good reason why they should not descend to earth, and give the assistance that they have too long withheld. They could build the cars to reinstate England in its old position; they have the men, they have the money, they have the material. There is no dearth of intelligence to design engine and chassis; no mysterious gadgets have revolutionised foreign models and made all competition a waste of time. There is no necessity to send English mechanics disguised as Italian peasants to listen at the keyholes of the Alfa-Romeo works; everything is above-board, and success waits only for those with the initiative to take it. Yet our manufacturers delay. They seem to be overawed by certain trade organisations whose object it is to prevent them building; but, more than this, their inertia is due to a mutual fear and jealousy that forbids any one to take the first step. I record this with much reluctance, but it has been chiefly responsible for the neglect of resources and the leaving of them to drift into obsolescence. As long as such obstinacy prevails, not the most optimistic of us – and I am an ardent pupil of the benefit-of-the-doubt school – can hold out any hope for motor racing in England. Even just before 1931, no British car won a big race, except at Le Mans, without the assistance of handicap; they were dependent for their chances on a start. So it has come to this, that we who pride ourselves on our sportsmanship, who minted the word and laugh at it on foreign lips, have no representation in one of the main departments of sport. Worse, we are the only great European country in this humiliating position. I have actually had to suffer the sympathy not only of my own friends, but of foreigners. They would welcome our return to the lists with open arms, and are unable to understand our absence. Soon this admiration for our racing, based on the memory of previous years, will turn to indifference and even, later, to contempt. Whenever we enter a car now in a big race abroad, we are welcomed none the less and everything done to ensure our comfort. But our cars are considered no more seriously than an omnibus would be; it is agreed from the beginning that they have no sort of chance of approaching anything near victory. On one occasion we surprised them; in the Grand Prix at Pau in 1930 – a race which I shall describe later – I drove a four-seater Bentley with a touring body among the special French sports models, and came in second. The enthusiasm with which we were met thrilled me, and made me keener than ever to have an English car capable of sweeping the board. But the cheers at Pau seem to have been our swan song; and when I look at my list of 1931 and 1932 races, I find that out of a total of 15, of which 7 were on the Continent and 4 in Ireland, I drove foreign makes – either Alfa-Romeo or Maserati – 11 times, 2 of the remaining 4 occasions being attempts on the lap record at Brooklands. When I look on the other side of the sheet at the results of these races, I find a melancholy comparison; both times that I drove a Bentley, omitting the record attempts, I retired, while in all the other 11 on foreign cars there were only 2 complete failures, and 3 wins. Why should anyone be expected to neglect such an experience with the two Italian machines, and deny himself all hope, of success out of deference to an unreasonable whim? I know that in saying this I have the sympathies of all other English drivers of any note. We have respected the claims of England as much as was possible, though there was no material hindrance – this, I think, critics might take into kindly consideration – to our migrating in shoals across the Channel and racing to our heart's content from April until October. Yet Sir Malcolm Campbell, among many others, has been attacked as if he had actually changed his name to Campbellini.

It is almost incredible, but I have actually been met with the amazing argument that we do not compete in Continental Grand Prix races because we have no Grand Prix cars, but that if we could be bothered to build them we should, of course, win – it is therefore not worth while building them, victory in theory being as good as victory in fact. I seem to remember the answer to this from my preparatory school days, but the whole idea implies a gesture rather like threatening your enemy with an empty gun, without containing such a good bluff.

The more serious arguments, though they are poor enough, are those proposed against the erection of the road-course; if it were erected, of course the manufacturers would be compelled to doff their mask of indifference. (It is hard to understand why they could not have united to provide a sum that would build a common team of three cars, and put an end to all this ineffectual noisy fighting among themselves).

The choice of districts is wide, and especially in the eastern counties, where there are little-used roads that a certain expense could turn into first-class courses. They would naturally be constructed on the principle of the Nürburg Ring, to be used for practice in most months of the year and hours of the day. The noise is an overrated obstacle, which has not given trouble to the Germans; I do not know if our English ears are supposed to be more sensitive, but we grow used in a very short time to London traffic and provincial trains and aerodromes. It is too small a molehill to raise into a mountain, when such an important issue is involved. But it is hardly less silly than the evergreen bugbear of traffic dislocation. I am sick of this tedious objection. There is no reason to suppose the English less efficient than the Irish police, who, in a far more thickly populated part of the world arranged the T.T. race to the convenience of all traffic in the neighbourhood. The dislocation is far worse in the Lord's Mayor Show or on Derby Day, when it is almost hopeless to try and reach any destination near London except those two; neither function, though not without much picturesque and sentimental appeal, have a fraction of a motor race's commercial use.

I shall find great trouble in persuading to my point of view nervous parents or conscientious schoolmaster; the very thought of a road-course will make them shudder and tremble for the welfare of their wards. They will imagine them tearing down main thoroughfares at 200 mph where before they only pictured 100, and forbid them to have anything to do with this effort to license road-hogging. Such, I feel, must be the first thoughts of many such people. But surely, if these wild young sparks were given a closed road, with all the usual bends and corners and hills, on which to indulge their mania, they would not want to court danger elsewhere; and in time they would acquire a skill and confidence to justify increased acceleration on main roads. I can say, without fear of contradiction, that the expert driver is the safest of all classes of motorist, and to reach his level should be the ambition of all who own fast cars. Though I do not agree with the man who races over cross-roads because the greater the speed, the less the chance of hitting another car, I think that an expert is no menace however fast he goes. I would far rather be with him than with scrupulous clerics clinging to the middle at a shy 25, or those ubiquitous thousands of women who are "just beginning." The expert has accustomed himself to high speed, and knows by instinct how to deal with a crisis. Only a road-course can make this familiarity universal. For there would, of course, be instructors, and the profession of driving racing cars would be taken into serious account. On the Continent it is already one of the most remunerative, and success may easily bring an income of £5,000 or £6,000 a year.

The firms themselves who build the cars would strive no longer in covert suspicion, but in open competition, and a great impulse be given to motor manufacture in the factories all over England. In Italy the team which wins the 1,000-mile race, or any of the big events, ensure to their car the command of next season's sales, and obtain a wide international publicity. I know for certain that in 1931 the Alfa-Romeos drew over £10,000 out of successes in the way of Prize Money and Bonuses.

Foreign money would come pouring into the country if a road-course were built in England; this is not merely my own theory, but an argument that anyone can corroborate. During the period of the T.T. race, there came to Belfast, in the week, over £80,000 of foreign money from England and elsewhere, and a crowd of over a quarter of a million attended. Consider the difficult journey to Belfast, however the railway and steamship companies may lighten it: two train journeys and a long unpleasant crossing. Then consider the ease with which an English course could be reached. Why must we be seasick to watch our road-racing? A bus or a short railway journey could land us at our English course, and crowds, tempted at last by a new attraction at their doors, would flock in far greater numbers, in millions, to the English race meetings. They would return again and again, as the foreigners return, and bring more with them, until the novelty became an institution, and excitement was leavened by intelligence in a desire to uphold the British motor market. The shops in the neighbourhood of the road would flourish, and their proprietors be able to retire after a few years; fame would crown the district and canonise it with St. Epsom and St. Stratford-on-Avon. But in commercial importance it would always be far greater than these. Foreigners would flock to it, instead of waiting for us to go to them, bringing the spirit of Kameradschaft or Fraternité; and international relations would be aided by a voluntary friendship far stronger than political entente. So it has always been on the Continent, and we would be no less eager, once the time came, to welcome our guests and parade the glories of our new circuit; and cars would be built once more to restore our honour.

How and who would build this great new course in England? We could not do better than copy the example of the Nürburg Ring, which was made for the express purpose of relieving unemployment. From 1925 to 1927 this measure did much to lighten the poverty to which Germany was then especially subject; the cost was contributed by local funds and government assistance, an action which neither the locality nor the government have had any reason to regret. They are beginning to make a large profit out of the frequent race meetings. We are not so rich in England that we can afford to neglect such opportunities; yet still our unemployment figures mount, and still no move has been made to relieve it in this way, and still our own English firms must take their cars abroad if they wish either to test or advertise them in the best way possible. They incur additional expense, and so slight is the interest of the public that they derive little benefit from their enterprise. Such is the apathy with which insults to one of our finest sports and leading industries are gazed on; but what a hullabaloo would be raised if the same treatment were dealt out to football or cricket. Righteous indignation would blaze in every column of every newspaper, if a famous football team were told to play all its matches away from home, and actually forbidden so much as to practise on its own ground. We would never hear the end of it, if our cricket side were sent to Australia, to prepare for a match that circumstances prevented from ever being played in England. Yet the parallel to the indignities which prey upon English motoring is accurately drawn.

Now let us pick bare the last bone of contention. I have a feeling that, with the end of every paragraph, some of my readers have been hungrily expectant to see how I should deal with this final point, and when still nothing was said, when it began to seem as if I was shirking, they could hold themselves in no longer and burst out with one accord, "But what about Brooklands? Brooklands, the home of British motor racing, the foster-mother of record-breakers, surely you cannot have forgotten Brooklands?" I have not forgotten Brooklands. But for some pages I have been wondering how I should best express my opinion of it. I think that it is, without exception, the most out-of-date, inadequate and dangerous track in the world. I shall lay myself open to much recrimination for saying this; but I know Brooklands well and that is my conclusion.

The layman, who does not make a habit of watching the races there, has an impression of the track gathered from passing it in the train. Admiring the huge banking with an unused and callow eye, and hearing the cars roaring when several miles away, he looks up to Brooklands as the Mecca of the motor world. It is nothing of the sort; it has only kept its importance so long because it has never had a rival in England since its creation. I say frankly that it could not have existed for more than a season in America or on the Continent, while we have been perforce satisfied with it for 20 years. There was undoubtedly a time, in the years before until the years shortly after the war, when it was a good track. But in recent seasons, it has failed even to provide the public with a good spectacle. A system of handicapping has been made essential, which affords the ludicrous sight of a car capable of 135 m.p.h. chasing round after a midget with a maximum of 105, and had the handicaps not been so brilliantly proportioned by Mr. Ebblewhite, the official starter, all public curiosity would have vanished years ago. I have, in common with the majority, a very great respect for Ebby, which I should like to place on record. He has rendered incalculable services to the B.A.R.C., to which any reward must be, and is, hopelessly inadequate. He has to work out handicaps sometimes to a fifth of a second, always remembering the psychology of the drivers, and that 'pulling' is no more foreign to the motor-racing than to the horse-racing world. He has discharged all his duties, and surmounted all his obstacles, with an ability responsible for about half the remaining attraction of Brooklands.

But even Ebby could not make up for all that was out of date in the track. Brooklands was built for speeds no greater than 120 m.p.h., and for anyone to go over 130, without knowing the track better than his own self, is to court disaster. The lap record is already nearly 140, and it is unlikely that speed will call a halt to further advance, and stagnate agreeably until we have a modern track to suit it. Meanwhile, those who wish to set a higher pace, as they have every reason for wishing, must risk their necks because there is nowhere else in England to go. The surface is abominable; to those who had never had any experience of it at high speed, it would be incredible. There are bumps, which jolt the driver up and down out of his seat and make the car leave the road and travel through the air. I am absolutely amazed that this has not caused far more fatal accidents. We are asked to race against the clock, which is not a condition of a proper motor race. Meetings at Brooklands can only be considered as a joke, if jokes may be combined with such attendant perils. It is pleasant to meet friends there at the beginning of the season, and hear their opinions of the past and prospects for the future; it is amusing to have a race or two, as long as they are not to be taken too seriously. But otherwise the place has become a farce. This is no new opinion of my own to cause a sensation, nor yet one held by me alone. The closer the intimacy with Brooklands, the more inevitable it appears. To the expense and risks taken the prizes are quite disproportionate; but people, anxious to mention some use which the track has not failed to serve, say that it makes an admirable nursery for young drivers. Even this is untrue. I am not deliberately setting up skittles because I know I can knock them down again, but reviewing all the possibilities of this overrated place, it is not enough to condemn the absence of a much-needed circuit, I must try and give a clear picture of what already exists. If I could find anything true to shed an attractive blur over all Brooklands' diseases, I would make use of it at once; but there is nothing at all. If young drivers were to learn there, they would have to find someone who could teach them. But there is no one. Every other great sport has its professionals, who willingly devote themselves to teaching in the service of their particular clubs. The very smallest village cricket grounds often have nets, and a groundsman to coach; but at Brooklands, the biggest, the only motor-racing ground in the land, there is not a soul. It is more important to the public safety that a man should be able to drive a fast car than hold a bat straight. At aerodromes there are teachers, and aeronautics have had far less time to complete their equipment than motor racing. So the young would-be driver has to go down to Brooklands, and detect all its difficulties for himself; without continual attention, if his car is not too fast, he achieves nothing except to keep his foot on the accelerator. But if he has a car capable of over 130 m.p.h., he is taking a very great risk indeed to drive it there, at that speed, in his first six months. There are in this, as in all sports, the right and the wrong way of playing; without teaching or experience the young driver cannot help playing it the wrong way. What makes his ignorance far more deadly in this than in any other game, is the terrible jeopardy in which it puts others. He fails to keep a straight course, he swerves suddenly, or goes too high on the banking. There are examples of novices committing these unpardonable crimes, and sometimes being fortunate – but at others they cause an accident, from which they may escape themselves, but which is dangerous to those behind. On a track such as Brooklands, with its bumps and idiosyncrasies to be learnt by heart, a teacher is essential to unskilled drivers. I took four years to venture on it at over 130, though certainly much of that time was spent in increasing my car's speed; but with my present car, three years ago, I should not have dared to attempt such a venture, nor been able, had I dared, to drive at its maximum with the smallest degree of safety. Yet suggestions are proposed to turn Brooklands into a road-track. Not only is the space at the designer's disposal far too limited for such an extension, but nothing associated with Brooklands could stand any comparison beside the great foreign circuits. It is generally agreed to be the worst possible influence for any one meaning to race on road-courses; it gives no kind of preparation for the difficulties of Belfast and Le Mans, and for a novice to go to one of these, when in apprenticeship, direct from Brooklands, is a thoroughly unwise and hazardous policy. The track's only possible use is as a testing ground for new cars, and a site for high speed reliability trials, provided that the speed never exceeds 110. In this role it would be almost invaluable; but in the role it strives to play now it is ludicrous.

So the inadequacy of Brooklands, and the absence of a road circuit, have put English prestige in very low water with the English who know the position. Their despair cannot fail to become more obvious yearly to the foreigners, whose estimation of our motor industry will sink in proportion, while there is no change in the apathy of our public. The *raison d'etre* of motor racing has been lamentably ignored in this country, and as no one will awake to its importance except those who are tired of emphasising it, we still have no road-circuit. It is a pity; for if we did succeed in gaining it, the organisation would be without fault, and popularity guaranteed from the start. For a little while there was the same despondence over our hopes for the Schneider Trophy; but at the last a most patriotic and sporting person promised to finance it with £100,000, and the race as a race was a complete farce; the Italian teams never appeared, but there is no chance of such a fiasco in the event of a road-circuit being built. Its first meeting would be attended by teams of foreigners who have been longing for such an occasion, and crowds would flock there more certainly than they do to Belfast. The longer I dwell on the subject, the more astounded I am that public enthusiasm has been so spasmodic. Horse-racing has a continuous appeal to the people, yet the majority do not own horses; motor-racing leaves them lukewarm, though most of them have motors. They have a greater use for motors; they do their business in them and employ them on the most urgent errands. They expect and get a high degree of efficiency out of them, which is only attained after the most searching tests in big races; yet they will do nothing towards having such tests held at home. Horses have not the great commercial use of cars; they do not carry national prestige so conspicuously; there is no huge international competition in the Derby or Grand National, nor is every part of a horse fitted in British factories. Yet horse-racing still exercises, by its beauty and excitement, the hold that motor-racing should have by virtue of both beauty, excitement and practical advantage. The only solution in which I take refuge, is that the English public is slow to substitute for its traditions the novelty of something useful.

It is so little to ask, either a team of three cars, of a road-circuit that will allow us to hold up our heads once more among foreigners. One would follow the other; and lest any person, horrified by my mention of the Schneider Trophy and £100,000, be inclined to exaggerate the cost, I give my word that £20,000 would cover all experimental and incidental expense, and build a team of three cars good enough to lead the world. Yet—if I can be forgiven flogging a dead horse—a subsidy of three times this sum was guaranteed to an art, which might have been equally essential to national prestige, but could never have given the same commercial remuneration. Opera is surely a delightful thing that can be shelved for a while, and taken down at will. But this question of motor-racing demands an immediate response; that is why

I have stated my own opinions and the facts without any pretence of concealment. I wish it to be clearly understood that they are the opinions of the majority of racing motorists, and that I have only been given a convenient moment to represent them to the public. Delay would have been disastrous, and the failure of even this present arraignment would be likewise disastrous. Success can only come from a definite proposal by some rich and enlightened person, whose name will be remembered with gratitude for ever, of, in an equal degree, by the inspiration of the public to take a more permanent and careful interest. With this to depend upon, the plans of the experts, that were in laborious preparation long ago, have a great hope of realisation. But there can be no waiting, no paroxysm of patriotic enthusiasm that is to disappear entirely with the end of the book. The cross-roads are reached now, offering the alternatives of continued lethargy and probably irretrievable loss of reputation, or of advance towards the recovery of prestige.

I am sorry if I have offended any one in any remark I may have made; but bluntness seemed the only means left, to impress on the public the importance of motor-racing to both industry and country.

— CHAPTER X —

First Year in Exile

I take this opportunity to mention a man who has never nagged in his devotion to motor racing, and continually given against misfortune an example of courage and determination. Sammy Davis is known to the motoring world hardly less for his accounts of the racing as for his own successes in it, and his book is one that every enthusiast should read. He is a fine driver undeterred by accidents to his team or to himself; and people will not readily forget his courageous victory after the White House crash at Le Mans in 1926. His performance there was typical of him; he brought his car past the post after it had been involved in the worst disaster of recent years, literally hauling it out of a holocaust of wrecks, and driving it to the finish without brakes. He regards a race as a crusade; he seems to devour it, and trains unflinchingly beforehand. He works on the fine principle of striving to finish, whatever the odds, and I think he would willingly shoulder his car and carry it to the post. If his enthusiasm could be cut up into small pieces and let into the brains of the public, we might come nearer our road-course without making very much difference to Sammy Davis.

I see that towards the end of 1930 the following headline announced the withdrawal of Dorothy Paget's support: *"Speed Queen Quits Racing."* But there were two more events that year, one of them the 500 mile at Brooklands, which found the single-seater in a bad mood and was spoilt by the handicaps given to small cars. But a cheerful end was made of a pessimistic season by the French Grand Prix at Pau. It took place in perfect weather before an enormous crowd, and stands vividly in my memory as the most interesting and thrilling race in which I have ever taken part. Its purpose was for stripped racing cars of the Bugatti and Delage type, and among these greyhounds my 4½-litre supercharged Bentley of Le Mans was like a large Sealyham. Its entry was regarded by the French as a sporting venture, and by their stern mechanics as a joke. It weighed 2 tons to the 20 hundredweight of the official Bugattis and Delages, and had a horsepower of 200 to their 160-190, while all the French cars were driven by men – among them their champion Louis Chiron – who knew the course better than their own bedrooms. I saw at once that my only chance lay in regaining on the straight what I was bound to lose on the bends, a task that turned out to be more arduous than I had supposed. My difficulties were complicated by two adventures which would have appeased a young novelist's passion for the unexpected. I was racing at 135 mph down the 6-mile straight in the wake of Louis Chiron's Bugatti, which was itself doing about 130. Chiron seemed to be having trouble of a sort, for his head was continually ducking into the cockpit as if he wanted to find something. As I came up to the rear of his car, it began slowly to swerve across the road, until for an instant my left front wheel was between his two back wheels. He still had his head in the cockpit, and there seemed no chance of avoiding a terrible crash. Of course, I sounded the horn for all I was worth, and then instinctively let out one of the loudest yells that can ever have been heard. It rose above the noise of my engine, and it rose above the noise of his. He looked up as if he had been shot, and switched his car over to the right-hand side of the road. The Bentley just scraped past.

It is the only mistake I have ever known Chiron make, and very nearly made a second impossible. I could not have failed to sweep straight through his tiny Bugatti, as if it had been a matchbox on wheels, and he admitted it after the race. His apologies were quite embarrassing; he had met with oil gauge trouble and did not know that I was anywhere near; he could not say how sorry he was. It would have been very hard not to forgive him, even if I had not wanted to, so charming was his manner and so polished his way of speech. I am glad that I was behind him on that occasion, because they say that every great man makes his mistakes, and, after seeing Chiron make his, I shall have complete confidence in him for the future.

But even then, the destiny which controlled that race did not consider my excitement sufficient, and arranged another little drama for my benefit. About half-way through the race I approached a turning which I was accustomed to take at 80; and when the car was just round it, I came upon a picture the memory of which, whenever it comes to my mind, takes me back to that moment I first saw it. On the right hand of the road was a wrecked Bugatti, and lying across the middle, face downwards and arms stretched rigid by his side, was the driver, with a pool of blood oozing from beneath his chin. I could not brake in time; if he was killed I would have to run over him, one death being better than two; but if he was not killed, there seemed to be no room between him and the edge of the road to stop me tearing into a deep ditch. The crowd was quite silent; no one shouted to me to tell me what had happened. I did not dare assume that he was dead, so I went through, not daring to look at the wheels on the side of the ditch; and I swear that the other wheels missed that man's head by less than two inches. When I stopped, I found a trace of blood on them. On the next lap I saw an ambulance moving away from the corner, and thanked my stars I had not made the other decision. The following day a lady came to my hotel in Pau, and asked to see me. She was the wife of the injured driver, who was now in the local hospital;

and after thanking me with many tears, she told me that her husband had been conscious the whole time, and saw quite clearly the wheels rushing at his head and heard the hissing sound as they went past. He confirmed my own belief that there were not two inches between them and himself. He raced under the name of Sabipa, and I met him the next year at the French Grand Prix. He shook me energetically by the hand, and thanked me for saving his life. But I cannot see that there was anything at work in his salvation except the very greatest of good fortune. I myself had no time to weigh the pros and cons.

The race had a suitably dramatic finish. There was only one car in front of me, a Delage driven by Étancelin, which I was rapidly overtaking. He had very little petrol left, and was afraid it would give out just before the finish. But I never caught him; he won by 3½ minutes, and passed the post with less than half a gallon in the tank, after a non-stop run. It was the last of all the big races in which I ever had any success with the old green Bentleys, and the most enjoyable. When it was over, Monsieur Faroux, the doyen of French motor racing, came up to me and said, "The crowd laugh at your Bentley, capitaine Birkin, but I tell them not to laugh. I have seen the Bentleys at Le Mans, and I know. I am Faroux. I am not a fool."

Nor was he.

Last of all, the crown was set on this most perfect of days by a dinner party that Pierre Merillion gave in our honour. He owns a beautiful chateau near Pau, with a genius in the kitchen and superb wine in the cellar; all of these he put entirely at our service, and provided the best evening after a race that I have ever spent.

It also set the climax on my 1930 season, and I was soon arranging to drive foreign cars.

1931 opened with a tragedy. Glen Kidston was killed in May, when his aeroplane crashed among the mountains on its African flight. In him England lost a man who should be an example to all young Englishmen of how to live. He was quite without fear; he lived bravely and he died bravely. A fine, but not a first-class driver, he was courageous beyond words. He went at everything that opposed him with his eyes open, and there was nothing too arduous for him to undertake. He was a loss to motoring, but a far greater to his country,

A little after the news of his death became known, the first meeting of the year was held at Brooklands. It was the Double Twelve Race, which I have already had occasion to describe as ridiculous. Its absurdity was even more marked this year, when a *crèche* of midgets were given such huge handicaps that no big car had the slightest hope of defeating them. This may sound a prejudiced point of view, when I say that I was forced to retire after two hours. But the race was won by a scuttling kindergarten of four M.G.s, which are very fine cars indeed, but could have done nothing else in the circumstances except win.

Compared with the fuss made about it, this event was such a farce that I see no object in describing it, except to mention the fine and reliable performance of the smaller British cars. Now that the opposition of the big makes, such as the Bentleys, was withdrawn, or at all events weakened until it was negligible, the small cars began, with the aid of their handicaps, to push their way to the front, and did a little to revive our fainting prestige on the Continent. But they could never be taken as serious competitors there, and their successes in England could not make up for our greater failures unaided. Their victory in this particular race was made the occasion of much self-vindication, by those who had refused to view our prospects for 1931 with pessimism. They worked themselves up into a great state of patriotic fervour, until they had a big enough supply to last them for the year, and swamp any subsequent misgivings. They were mostly people who came to watch motor racing for the spectacle, members of the unmechanically minded public; and they could not penetrate beneath the glamour of victory to see what it really meant. I know that this attitude in the tyro is a very difficult one to prevent; but I state, for what it is worth, that the finest effort in any race is not necessarily made by the man who wins it. There is luck to be considered, both the good luck of the winner himself and the bad luck of his opponents. There are the circumstances, the time the cars have had for preparation, the fitness of their drivers, and the condition of the weather.

Above all is the handicapping, which causes the greatest distortion of view.

On May 25th there was another, the Whitsun meeting, at Brooklands, and this I seem to have made the occasion of further controversy about the inadequacy of the track and the absurdity of the handicap races. I have already said all I had to say, but this meeting roused me to particular rage owing to the attitude in which the lay spectators prepared to watch. They thought about it as a "fine holiday" to watch the cars "leaping through the air" over the disgraceful bumps on the surface, until the drivers were not quite sure whether or not they were acrobats at a circus. The public were tempted with the bait of "real excitement" and "spectacular thrills," and given very little chance to regard the race as serious, or the sport of which it was meant to be an example. I heard people of abysmal ignorance telling each other that it would be a "real test" if I could win the Gold Star Handicap, when I knew quite well that it would be impossible. A swarm of less fast cars than my single-seater – which was making its first appearance on the track for that year – were entered with large handicaps, and I was to give John Cobb a start of five seconds in his Delage. He is one of the finest of Brooklands drivers; but had he been a half-wit he would have been forced to go so high on the banking to pass the little cars, that there could have been no room for me. So in spite of the single-seater, which ran beautifully, I had a depressing meeting, nothing more than an endless round of useless jolts and bumps. But for others it was more pleasant, and I was very glad that Francis Howe won the Gold Star Handicap, averaging 120. Malcolm Campbell drove the Blue Bird round for two laps, and was greeted with great applause, but the crowd was a little disappointed that it did not travel at several hundred miles an hour, not being aware that the surface of Brooklands is less good than the sands of Daytona. Just before the fifth race a magnificent sight was seen, though only a few appreciated it in full. Two superb Bentleys were observed moving up to the Fork into their official positions, at the wheel of each sat a steward, who had retired a few years before from the leadership of those who race to the leadership of those who control racing, and was now about to signify approval that the event should start – no less celebrities than Bill Guinness and Bertie Moir.

In less than a month Le Mans had returned, but there was no Bentley to greet it. I was driving a 2-litre straight-eight Alfa-Romeo with Lord Howe, and the colour of the car was red and not the familiar green. This event stands in my memory as a pageant of colour; the streets before the race and the grandstands during it were like the lists in an old tournament. Every man had the favour of his hero's car in his tie or his sweater or his cap, and some of the young Frenchmen even walked about in overalls copied as a dress from a fashion plate. Lord Howe wore a red carnation in his cap, but had not given up his famous blue symphony. He drove beautifully during the whole time he was in the car, steering it safely during the most difficult hour of the race, when a thunderstorm passed in the night and made the road into a river. The two Mesdames, Mareuse and Siko, who had done so well to qualify in 1930, were once more in their Bugatti. They wore peacock-blue tunics, and were disqualified for coming in to refuel after 18 instead of after 20 laps. This was unfortunate for them. Our Alfa-Romeo ran very well after we had mended a little plug trouble, and exceeded the record distance of 1930 by 125 kilometres, at 78.13 mph, which was also a record. But the race was marred by a tragedy at that old scene of tragedies, Mulsanne Corner, among the trees, where the crowds gather by the right-angle bend. Rost in his Bugatti was racing towards it at well over 110 when a tyre burst, and the car left the ground, flying across the road into the spectators in the wood. They were so closely packed at this point that nothing could save them but luck; a man was killed, and another very seriously injured, while the car was wrecked against a tree. But neither Rost nor his mechanic were hurt fatally, and I heard that Rost left the scene moaning, "Why was it not I that was killed?" But the crowds that go to the most dangerous corners must be considered responsible for their own safety, and, though I have no wish to belittle the disaster, I hold the victims to blame, if blame can be attached to anyone.

The sweets of victory were to be embittered still more; I was thinking how much greater my satisfaction would have been in a Bentley instead of an Alfa-Romeo, when a telegram arrived from Mussolini, congratulating Francis Howe and myself on our success –"for Italy."

Le Mans was followed by Montlhéry, where I had not previously driven. I entered a Maserati with George Eyston and we managed to finish fourth. He was an ideal partner for this event, because he has an intimate knowledge of both road and track racing, and the Montlhéry circuit is a combination of the two. His driving is very scientific, for he is a skilled mechanic as well as driver, who cannot take enough pains over the preparation of his car. His successes and records with baby cars are too famous to rehearse. He is never perturbed, and on one occasion during this race was in dire need of all his composure. The roads had become very slippery and every one was finding his seat almost intolerably uncomfortable; Varzi I think drove with a cushion at his back, and another driver called desperately for padding. I lost a large patch of skin which did not return for several weeks. But all of these were able to shield their discomfort with a screen of polite discretion, and, more important, the seat of their trousers. George Eyston was less fortunate; he lost the latter, and found it very hard after that to keep the former. We had stopped at the pits, and he was bending over the engine in front of the grandstands, when suddenly a roar of laughter rose from the ranks of Frenchmen. At first neither of us could understand the reason for it, and we looked up and down the course for a source of amusement. By their signs and cat-calls the delighted crowd soon betrayed George's disaster, but not until he himself had betrayed a liberal area of his person to them. This did not prevent him from driving a very fine race, though we could not keep up with Chiron and Varzi who won. The public were in a very good humour all that day and greeted the English drivers with loud approval. I am not surprised that they were pleased, remembering the comedy that occurred before the start. The charabanc containing all the officials of the race had a breakdown, so that none of them could arrive until it was too late. The French spectators, taking this very good and unforeseen chance, ran amok in the grandstands; they parked their cars wherever they wished and sat in the seats preserved for the mighty. Their particular favourite among the foreigners was the Lord Earl Howe, who was driving a Bugatti with Brian Lewis. They finished twelfth, which was a fine effort after wasting an hour and a half at the pits.

George Eyston bought a new pair of trousers and drove with me a few weeks later in the Twenty-four Hour Endurance Race at Spa. We were on an Alfa-Romeo, and led by forty minutes in eight hours when we broke down. But we resolved to stay at Spa for another week and revenge ourselves in the Belgian Grand Prix. But we obviously could not enter the standard four-seater Alfa, that had been correct for the twenty-four hour event, in a race for properly stripped racing cars. So we had set to work to convert it in the few days between the two meetings, when George Eyston was compelled to return to England. I immediately cabled Brian Lewis to ask him if he would take the empty place, and on the Wednesday night he arrived. The race was on Sunday; with a little help and "scrounging" of certain parts from the Alfa-Romeo team, and by dint of removing every unessential nut and bolt, we managed to have our private car ready on Friday night. When I took it out in practice, it was still giving trouble; and Brian Lewis was forced to acquire as much knowledge as he could of a strange course on a 6-litre closed saloon Bentley. He was able to use the Alfa on Saturday; but when I handed over to him after my first relay in the race itself, I felt great anxiety. He had very little experience of Alfa-Romeos, being accustomed to cars of an entirely different kind, and he could not have had time to become intimate with the course. But he drove one of the finest races I have ever seen. I had impressed upon him that our only hope of finishing high up depended on keeping the car out of the ditch, as we had little chance of clinging to the official Alfas and Bugattis and Mercedes.

Most of the world's best drivers were driving the world's best makes. But Brian never looked like yielding his place; as he felt more at home with the car, his lap speeds began to increase until at the end of his turn he was improving on mine. Owing to his efficiency, we were able to creep into fourth place, which we kept until the end. Misfortune robbed

Nuvolari of victory when his friends were just preparing to lead him in in triumph; with two laps to go, his second driver, Borzacchini, drew alongside the pits, complaining that there was a fault in the petrol supply. Nuvolari leapt over the counter, and after furious adjustments, rushed off to catch Williams' Bugatti which had passed him. His combination of speed and skill in those last two laps were the admiration and wonder of all; he drove like a demon, but never gave any idea of recklessness, and his failure by seconds was thoroughly undeserved. Campari, too, was most unlucky. He had only to complete the course that day to become champion driver of Europe; he could have wandered round at his leisure, averaging 10 mph, had he wanted, and it was agreed that he should make no effort to win the race. But when he had completed his turn at the wheel, and the second driver taken over, a stone from a car in front was flung up through the oil sump, so that the Alfa could not continue. It was the only Alfa that met this fate; but Campari accepted his disappointment in a very sporting way, seeking the consolation of a large meal and exclaiming during the bites, "It could not be helped – it could not be helped."

From Spa we went to Nürburg, completing a sort of grand tour of the continental courses. I finished tenth on a Maserati and Lord Howe eleventh on a Bugatti; but disappointment finds it is hard to rankle on a course like this. I say, without hesitation, that it is the best in the world, and to it all the world's best drivers had foregathered. It was a battle on Olympus. Chiron was the god for France, Carraciola for Germany, Nuvolari for Italy, while the last two were due to fight their duel, which Carraciola's disqualification at Belfast in 1930 had postponed. In the middle of the race there was a storm of rain, putting Carraciola in his element. He had a struggle to keep his lead over Chiron, who was overtaking him on every one of the 22 laps; but he won by little more than a minute to the great satisfaction of the German crowds. They were stirred a little from their scientific calm that day, as who would not be, seeing Carraciola, Chiron, Varzi and Nuvolari finish on each other's heels with about five minutes between them?

Beside these giants' courses, Brooklands is like a toy; but I came back for the August Bank Holiday Meeting, in time to be unplaced from scratch once more. I averaged 75.21 for a lap of the Mountain course, of 12 miles with 20 hairpins, and 71.38 for a race, both of which were records and both quite unavailing. I made an attempt on Kaye Don's lap record of 137.58, which it was among my dearest ambitions to beat, but the wind had risen too high, and I never reached more that day than 136.45. There was a large and enthusiastic crowd; but I missed the intelligence of the foreigners more sharply in proportion to the month I had just spent on their roads. There did not sound in the English applause the same depth. The note of appreciation was not there, and at times a silence fell that was full, not of sympathy, but of sheer boredom. In moments of thrill it was a pleasure to be among my own people again, but during the long spells that are inevitable, when no one is rushing along the edge of the banking or flying through the air, their attitude was most discouraging. I drove the red 4½-litre single-seater Bentley, which belonged, of course, to Dorothy Paget, though her active interest had ceased. But when the T.T. race came round again, there was still no English car for me to drive.

A horde of small machines had entered, among them as many as twelve M.G. Midgets, which were given a handicap prohibitive to other people's chances. Big cars, realising how very hard it would be to see any hope against these odds, had entered in far fewer numbers, and the race thereby lost not a little of its previous attraction. Lord Howe and I were driving Alfas of our own, while the official team was under the charge of Nuvolari, Campari and Borzacchini, three of Italy's leading drivers, and Nuvolari, the greatest in the world. Before the race a telegram arrived from Mussolini ordering them to win, a command they were obviously not eager to disobey. They very nearly missed reaching Belfast entirely. I found them at Euston Station, gesticulating and shouting to a group of anxious officials, and trying to make their object understood; but when they saw the capitano Birkin, they made a dash for me and forced me to explain that they were going to Ireland, which I was very glad to do. But I still think I missed a great opportunity of having them sent to the Isle of Mull.

The Talbots had also entered, and were contemplating the non-stop run which was now almost expected of them; a very fine display indeed was given in one of them by Brian Lewis, who had no trouble at all, averaged 77 and came in fourth. Brian is quite the most light-hearted motorist I know; he fills the position of jester. He never appears to have any concern in his races, yet has managed to acquire a more than average knowledge and skill. He is the master of cornering and one of the most reliable of drivers.

On the Friday I had my last practice, while the Italian manager, Ferrari, and their great designer, Jano, sat behind locked doors, guarded by a mechanic, discussing and revising their tactics for the morrow. The race had an amazing start, the various batches of cars starting off at intervals, some with a lap or more of handicap and others with only a few minutes, representing a fraction of a lap; but one driver showed complete contempt of this system, Victor Gillow, who ran up a bank at the first corner and completed no laps at all.

I was placed at the start behind all three official Alfa-Romeos, as well as the one Francis Howe was driving. But before the race their designer, Jano, told me, perhaps out of kindness, perhaps for an unknown reason, "We make our cars go slow the first two laps to warm the oil." Profiting from this, I warmed my oil before the start and passed all three Italians on the first lap. I do not think they were pleased. My

Clement, Davis, Benjafield, Rubin, Barnato and Birkin stand by their Le Mans Bentleys in Mayfair - Courtesy Brooklands Motor Museum

Birkin at 1930 Grand Prix de L'ACF Pau. 20th September 1930 - The Geoffrey Goddard Collection

Second place for Birkin at 1930 Grand Prix de L'ACF Pau in his 4½-litre supercharged "Blower Bentley" touring car, stripped down to racing trim, with headlights and mudguards removed - The Geoffrey Goddard Collection

A second win at Le Mans in 1931 with Earl Howe racing the Alfa Romeo 8C 2300 LM - The Geoffrey Goddard Collection

Birkin in Alfa-Romeo 8C 2300 LM at 1931 TT -
The Geoffrey Goddard Collection

Birkin stands up in his Bentley as it catches fire at 80 mph. 30th September 1931.
Courtesy Brooklands Motor Museum

Birkin, Gallop and Harcourt Wood in Brooklands pits. 500 Mile event 1931 - Courtesy Brooklands Motor Museum

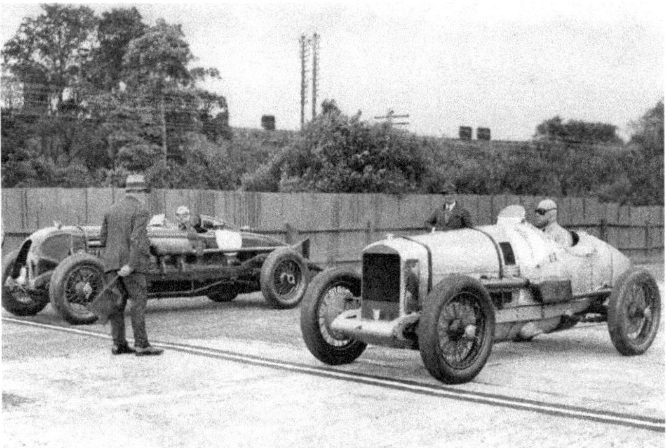

Birkin and John Cobb line up before their 1932 head-to-head - Courtesy Brooklands Motor Museum

Practice run at 1932 Easter Meeting - Courtesy Brooklands Motor Museum

With fellow driver Bernard Rubin prior to the Tripoli Grand Prix. 7th May 1933 - Courtesy Brooklands Motor Museum

Alfa actually broke the standing record with a speed of 77.3, on the next the lap record with 79.7, on the next with 80.09, and on the next with 80.48. But the Italians had no intentions of being out of the fun and leaving their own cars to set up new records under English hands; Campari on the very next round did 80.7, and about twelve laps later Borzacchini brought it up to 81.28. When Nuvolari retired, the Alfa-Romeo team was considering the idea of Borzacchini, who was only third string, giving up his car. But the officials made up their minds for them, by refusing to allow any such irregularity. About this time something began to unsettle the Italians in the pits, increasing their agitation with every lap, until at the end they were near apoplexy. They did not seem equipped to regard with calm the unexpected things that happened to their team. I had a great race with Campari and Borzacchini, and after two hours was leading on handicap. I drew in to refuel, and wasted some precious seconds over a front axle that had been bent out of line. As I drew out after 1 minute 58 seconds Campari passed me, but himself had to stop for fuel on the next lap. He only took 51 seconds, but as he restarted, I repassed him, with Borzacchini in another Alfa at my heels. We went up to Comber together, and as we approached the narrow street I thought I would try the licensed subterfuge of leading them down the garden path; this is done by braking a fraction of a second before the usual time, a difference that can change the whole aspect of a race by forcing the car behind, seeing it has overjudged its speed and the time at its disposal to get past, to run up an escape road, if there is one, or else crash. But instead of leading the Italians up the garden path, I found they were much too quick for me. There are few tricks of the trade they have not at their finger tips – and was led up it myself. The car crashed on to the sandbanks at Comber, and though I was able to go on for a little while, I was out of the race in theory and soon forced to be in fact. The finish was one of the most thrilling I have ever watched – I hope I may not have the opportunity of watching too many more – when Borzacchini, who had passed Campari and more than justified his right to continue instead of Nuvolari, was struggling to overtake the two M.G. Midgets. With two laps to go it was obvious that one of the Midgets must win on its handicap of five laps, but the other, with the same handicap, was only 2 minutes 59 seconds in front of the Alfa-Romeo; in the Alfa pits pandemonium broke loose, blackboards were waved, screaming Italians crimson in the face leant over the counter, jumped on to the track and shook their fists at the innocent little M.G. On the last lap Borzacchini was a minute and a half behind. "Avanti! Avanti!" yelled his supporters, and in the Alfa pits nothing was left standing, spare parts, petrol cans, blackboards all were overturned as the team waited for the cars to come into the straight for the last time. In the M.G. pits the mechanics were straining their eyes down the road, and making determined calculations. The first M.G. won to applause; and then the two came up towards the stands together, and almost on the post Borzacchini rushed past to be runner-up by 5 seconds. I have never seen any excitement to equal that of the Alfa-Romeo team; it was quite indescribable. The shadow of Mussolini does shed a very great and wide influence.

Among the gentlemen of note in the motoring world who make Belfast their especial pitch, is one who no longer races, and only goes round the road in an official capacity. This is Bill Guinness, whose admirable discharge of his duties is among the chief blessings of most big events in the British Isles. He was, in my opinion, about five years ago the finest driver that we possessed, and it is a source of regret that he should have retired. The tremendous difficulties of management never seem to upset him, he remains helpful and considerate throughout them all, and I have, among many others, the following good reason for supposing he does not take them in too pompous a spirit. In Ulster in 1929 he was given the position of Flying Marshal, a technical term in the official's vocabulary implying a heavy burden of duties to fulfil; and for his assistance he was lent one of the green Le Mans Bentleys, to take him to various points on the course and see that subordinate Marshals were doing their job. During the race I saw such a green Bentley some way in front half-hidden in a cloud of dust, and could not recall which member of our team it was. So I accelerated and began to give chase; but I found it was going as fast, and even faster than me. Whoever was driving was certainly putting his foot down; I did not seem to be gaining on him at all. Then he began to slow down, and I thought to myself maliciously that he must have engine trouble and deserved to if he intended maintaining that speed the whole way. As I passed, Bill Guinness waved from the cockpit; and 1 have never been persuaded that he was not enjoying a very good private race of his own.

The Belfast T.T. was held on August 22nd; not till October 3rd did I have another big engagement. This was the 500 mile race at Brooklands, which had been rendered so farcical in the previous year by the huge handicaps allowed to baby cars. There seemed no prospect of any improving alteration being made in the rules; but in spite of their long starts, the members of the kindergarten did not have such a conspicuous success. Jack Dunfee and Cyril Paul won on a 6-litre Bentley, a very fine victory; my own Alfa-Romeo was second at one time, and averaging over 122 on the lap, when the battery terminals came adrift and I had to draw in. This lost me my chance. Finally, and a few minutes before the finish, I had to withdraw altogether. But however blatant the absurdity of this event as a serious race, I cannot deny its great advantages as a test – indeed, I am very glad to find some compliment up my sleeve. The object of a motor race – though I repeat it at the risk of diffuseness – is to combine good racing with benefit to the industry; it is an achievement to have fulfilled half this purpose. The stress to which all the cars during the 500 miles were submitted, both by the struggle against handicap and the unevenness of the surface, should have given their makers much material for thought. Many of the smaller cars were unequal to it; their withdrawal was more than half responsible for the Bentley's victory, which I have no desire to belittle. It is to be supposed – and consequences proved it so – that the causes of these failures were investigated, and steps taken to avert them in the future. But the advance of the pygmies does not compensate the stagnation of the giants, and though a Bentley ran, no car of that size which would be equal to a foreign road-course made its appearance for trial. British tyres, however, were used by every competitor, and not a single burst recorded. It is worth adding that the Bugatti crash at Le Mans, which was due to bad tyres, occurred on the first occasion that a foreign make had been substituted, and this announcement, coupled with the resignation of the Bugatti team, drew forth a chorus of hissing from the French crowds. Yet although the considered preference of a foreign tyre is far less shameful than that of the whole of the foreign car, none but a desultory resentment has been shown in this country; our public has not given tongue to sincere patriotic indignation, because its interest is too casual and its information too superficial. I cannot help finding, in every Brooklands meeting, a pretext to reinforce and recapitulate the objections that have been previously raised, and I foresee a danger of my own plant being blighted with too much attention.

The winning Bentley averaged 118 miles per hour, an exceptional speed, which even then only just exceeds my limit of 110, suggested in the event of Brooklands being devoted entirely to speed trials. I can recall little else in the meeting, except a moment in the middle of a race, when a telegraph boy, whether or not from a conscientious urge to run his errands by the quickest possible route, was on the point of crossing the track on a bicycle. His zeal, or lunacy, or love at first sight, or whatever prompted the strange desire, was checked in time by an unsympathetic steward.

The few days before this race were not without their thrills. More than anything, I was keen to beat Kaye Don's record for the flying lap of 137.58 mph; our rivalry was of a long standing – I had previously beaten his old record, upon which he had at once beaten mine, but about four days before the 500 Mile I equalled him, and made up my mind to do better on the morrow. But on the morrow, when I was coming off the Byfleet Banking at about 130, the auxiliary petrol tank caught fire and flames began to lick the legs of my overalls. In later editions of the story, these flames have been exaggerated into a fiery furnace, and myself glorified into a sort of Shadrach, Meshach or Abednego. This is a corruption of the truth; but the cockpit certainly did become rather hot. So I switched off the engine and put on the brakes;

but before the car stopped I had to climb out of the seat and, perched on the back of the car, steer as best I could from a crouching position. I jumped off once it was safe and put out the fire. But the cockpit and my hands were both burnt, though it was not long before they were all right again. Once more I failed of the record by a fraction of a mile. In a fortnight's time I tried again at the Autumn Meeting, this time in a Maserati. I won the Mountain Championship, repeating my own lap record of 75.21. But when I attacked Kaye Don's record of 137.58, I could not even reach 137. So here was another feud to wait until next season.

— CHAPTER XI —

The Last Lap

The year 1931 had other escapades, unconnected with cars; whereat I hear a breath of relief rippling through the bosom of my audience. This I shall at once stifle by observing that if the story is unconnected with cars, it is none the less concerned with engines.

At the beginning of August, I decided to go to Paris by the new airplane, Hannibal, which had been built for Cross-Channel and Imperial routes and was the first of a fleet. We left Croydon after some delay, and over Tonbridge found ourselves enveloped in a rainstorm and thick fog. There were about twenty passengers on board, but most of them were men, and the pilot was Captain Dismore. He had already made a name by the adroitness with which he directed the passengers of an air-liner that fell into the sea in 1926. Hannibal had four propellers, and 25 minutes out of Croydon, one of them broke, its motor stopping instantly. Black smoke began to pour out of the engine, and part of the propeller which had broken off hit the tail. Dismore at once decided to land; he never lost his head, to which his landing is a testimony. Just clearing a roof-top, he brought the huge machine down into a small field. The whole of the tail was torn off on telegraph wires and all four engines were broken. One or two of the women were a little frightened, but I told them they were safe, as long as they allowed their bodies to lie limp. No one showed real agitation, and I think Dismore saved all our lives. The calm and presence of mind which all displayed were most remarkable in such a crisis, and most of us went on from Lympne aerodrome to Paris.

I have not yet described the Phoenix Park race, which was held in June. I was going to drive a 2366 c.c. straight-eight Alfa-Romeo, which Clive Gallop went to the Milan works to fetch. But when he got there he found the car not ready, and the factory so closely guarded, for Schneider Trophy work, against intruders, that he could convince nobody of his honesty. Luckily Mussolini heard of the difficulty, and, saying that the honour paid by an Englishman in driving an Italian car must be returned, commanded a special gang to prepare the Alfa in time. This was done, but Clive was not out of the wood when he left Milan on his return journey. The Italian frontier, closed on Sundays, was opened for him, but he was stopped at the French frontier; the car had no number plate and he had no papers. Once more official influence aided him; a French Brigadier of Customs improvised a cardboard number plate, and let him through. The car was driven to Holyhead on arrival, 330 miles covered in under 6 hours, and appeared in Dublin, after a journey worthy of the Three Musketeers, in time for one day's practice. It was a wonderful machine, prepared, in spite of hustling, with customary Italian thoroughness, much lighter, of course, than the Bentleys, and capable of about 115 mph.

The most coveted prize was the Phoenix Park Trophy, awarded on the best time of the two days under handicap. Norman Black on the first day had won the under 1500 c.c. class with 3 hours 21 minutes 20 seconds in an unsupercharged M.G. Midget. There was also, of course, a separate prize for the second day for those over 1500 c.c. Francis Howe was driving a Mercedes, and George Eyston and Campari Maseratis.

There were only ten starters. In the first half-hour Francis Howe broke the lap record twice at 91.8 mph, over Carraciola's 91.3 in 1931. He was leading, followed after 10 laps by Campari one second behind, George Eyston two seconds behind Campari, and myself five seconds behind George. The rain was beginning to come down in torrents; it was a day for the ducks and Carraciola. George lost six minutes changing plugs and refuelling; Campari's cornering was fast and skilful, but very Italian. He was trying to pass me, when a small stone kicked up by my wheels, struck his goggles, breaking the glass, which was not Triplex, and cut his eyeball. When he reached the pits, after driving in great pain, he handed the car over to Ramponi, and himself to a waiting specialist. The eye was treated, and with bandages swathed round his forehead, he took over as soon as it was possible. I was leading at 25 laps, with Francis second after three more. George Eyston had fallen to seventh, and for a little while the rain stopped. Then, after driving a fine race, Francis found that his supercharger was failing, and with it went his chance of victory. At 40 laps I spent 47 seconds refuelling. Campari was hot on my trail, thirsting to catch up lost time. The rain began again, and his bandages began to slip over the injured eye, but they did not abate his speed. B. O. Davis was third in a Mercedes; his cornering in the rain was one of the finest things in the whole race. At 45 laps I was given signals to increase my speed, as the Maseratis were gaining. George Eyston was now fifth, behind Brian Lewis who gave his usual display of brilliance and safe driving on a Talbot. In the next 5 laps, George gained 1 minute 11 seconds, and Campari 50 seconds on my Alfa-Romeo. But with 2 laps to go, I was 13 minutes ahead; at this rate, I thought, I shall win the Phoenix Park Trophy as well as the cup for the second day.

It was a vain conceit. We had just passed Mountjoy Corner; but when I put my foot on the accelerator, there was a tired cough from the engine and nothing happened. My heart sank – the Birkin luck again! My Italian mechanic thought the handbrake had stuck and, seizing it violently, let it go with a bang. He spoke no English, but luckily, in my limited Italian vocabulary, were the two words, "Niente Benzina." I used them, and they seemed to act as a sort of "Open Sesame"; the car spluttered on, managing to stagger into the pits. There we found every one with a face so long that they might have been in a Hall of Mirrors. They had heard the wireless croaking that I was missing badly at Mountjoy Corner, and had then begun to cork up the champagne. Then they heard "Birkin has stopped," and then, imagining the worst calamities, "Birkin is coming slowly to the pits." When I arrived, I could only shout one word, "Petrol!" and Gaboardi, the mechanic, had our tank filled in an instant. So we won the race for the second day, but lost the Phoenix Park Trophy by 13 seconds.

Campari was second, a courageous effort after such an unpleasant injury; yet in spite of such conquests on the road, he has not abandoned his passion to sing in grand opera. Brian Lewis was third in his Talbot, followed by George Eyston in his Maserati, and the two Mercedes with Francis Howe, who had looked so like winning, and B.O. Davis only a minute behind him. The race was a success with all, and Norman Black was presented with the Phoenix Park Trophy. Mr. Morris, of the Maserati works, said that the event must take place next year, even if he had to guarantee it himself, and it was agreed to be a financial as well as a sporting triumph.

But somehow or other it was not repeated next year, which is the same 1932 whose going will shortly be a source of pleasure to everybody. As I wade through my Sargasso of Press cuttings, I find very few races of this past season with much humour or personal interest to enliven a cold analysis. Lack of imagination, or distrust of falsehood, forbid me to invent incident, and most of the circuits should now be too overworked to suffer another description. I do not suggest that the motor-racing events of 1932 were dull, but that they were all without any great charm for me, except the lap-record match against John Cobb at Brooklands. The Ulster T.T., in many ways a very good race, was spoilt for me by the certain knowledge that I had no hope of victory. The course was crawling with the shoals of minnows that now seem inevitable, and the prize went to a 1089 c.c. Riley driven by C. R. Whitcroft. George Eyston was second in the same kind of car, and Hall third in an M.G. Midget. All these cars ran and were run with the greatest skill, the winner averaging about 2 mph more than Carraciola in his 7-litre Mercedes in 1929. This performance deserves high praise, though the weather conditions were better this year and the cars stripped of hoods, mudguards, lamps, and windscreen. The big cars were much missed; I think there is a moral in the fact that Francis Howe and I drove the only foreign cars, two straight-eight 2336 c.c. supercharged Alfa-Romeos, and that there was no class more powerful than ours. There were 30 laps, and in all the 60 that Francis and I covered that day, we broke Borzacchini's 1931 record of 10 minutes 5 seconds thirty-eight times. Francis averaged 80.53

and I 79.79 mph. His fastest lap was done at 82.65, and mine at 83.2, which was a record. But neither of us could defeat our handicap.

I took Humphrey Butler with me as my mechanic, an office he discharged with the assurance of an expert. He had the ideal temperament; he knew what he had got to do before he did it, and what it was for while he was doing it. He never lost his head, nor attempted everything at once. But on one of our stops while he was filling up, he spilt some petrol out of the can, as is inevitable on these occasions. A drop or two fell on me, but his own overalls were soaked. Few of my readers may be in the habit of drenching themselves with benzol but they will probably have some experience of iodine, which does not smart so much nor half so long. There were nearly three hours more of the race, and for all that period Humphrey must have been in agony. I could see him squirming as the petrol stung his flesh, which was badly burnt for some time afterwards. But he never complained, nor suggested pulling up for anything to ease the pain. He realised that his own interests must be subordinate to the team's, and without a great familiarity of the motoring world, in which courage is regarded as a matter of course, he gave a display of it that would have been conspicuous in a hardened professional.

I have astounded recollections of a certain Freddie Dixon, a great man in the motor-cycling world, who made his official debut on a racing car that day. His reputation was that of an audacious, undeterred and skilled driver, three epithets I see no room to criticise. He seemed to have no deep respect for corners which still perplexed the veterans; he laughed at bugbears, and swore at his car if it seemed reluctant or surprised. He at once became the centre of attraction, and in practice, on a strange course, with an experience obtained in a different world, without much fuss or ado proceeded to beat his class record by about 2 m.p.h. He did 74.17 on an 1100 c.c. Riley. In the race itself, he set a pace with which no one attempted to keep up for four hours, and was then passed by Whitcroft. This he could not tolerate; he dashed at Mill Corner at an indignant and impossible speed, hit the inside kerb, bounced off to the outside, put on the brakes, hit the bank, shot six feet in the air, cleared a large hedge, and then vanished. Crowds rushed to the scene, to find Dixon, Riley, mechanic and all, lying in a garden. The Riley was a little bent; the mechanic, I think went to hospital with a bad face; but Dixon did not seem to be unsettled. He may have had a few bruises. I should have enjoyed watching him win.

On reading the proofs of my 1931 Ulster race, I have found a curious omission of the printers. I was about to insert a story about Bertie Moir, but as I could not recall all the details, I left a blank, and continued, "This is one of Bertie's favourite stories." The printers, from a righteous disgust, let into this blank three large query marks, which give the impression of being the story's relics after expurgation;

but loth to impute anything questionable to Bertie's favourite stories, I have corrected the error and here take up the thread.

I told him, when we were practising, that he could take Dundonald Bridge at 3,200 revolutions. The next morning, before anyone else, he started out on his practice run without me, determined to go cautiously because he had not driven for six years and thought he was rather frightened. He arrived at Dundonald ready to rev. up to 3,000 and no more, found that he could not approach 3,000, braked hand and foot, and squeezed through at 2,400. The next lap he managed 2,500, the next tried higher and nearly flew off the course. He was upset at first, because he thought he had lost his cunning. He wondered humbly at my Herculean strength, and came in to find that my time was only three seconds better than his. "Yes," I said, "I was trying." He asked me what revolutions I got at Dundonald and I told him that it was best to rev. up to 4,000 at the end of the straight before cutting out. He went quite pale. "I knew it," he told himself, "I've lost my touch." Diffidently he asked me if I truthfully got 4,000 at Dundonald on top gear. I thought he had lost his wits. He stood there, quite a pathetic figure, solemnly confessing that he had tried 4,000 at Dundonald on top, when I told him clearly – and then it suddenly occurred to me . . . did I tell him, was I sure I told him that one had to change into third?

Poor Bertie! I suppose it was very vague of me.

The foreign races this year have been, from my point of view, disappointing. I went on a sort of grand tour with Francis Howe, and had no correspondingly grand success. Le Mans was duly attacked in the middle of June; but the passing of the Bentleys seems to have involved the loss of Le Mans. It is no longer our dominion. This year the Italian flag was set there in place of the English, and there was jubilation in the Alfa-Romeo works. We drove a 2337 c.c. Alfa ourselves, but had to retire at three in the morning with a cylinder head gasket broken.

Before the race, the whole of the crowds of spectators stood for one minute in silence. This was their tribute to Andre Boillot, a fine French driver, who had died after an accident in the previous week. There was a very bad accident about three-quarters of an hour after every one had sat down again, but nobody was killed. Once more the scene was the malicious White House Corner near Mulsanne, where the Bentley crash of 1927 was staged; two of the Alfa-Romeos were involved, one of them driven by Marinoni, who had been setting a tremendous pace; in the second lap he averaged 84 mph, and in the fifth lap 86. He had an eventful day, and if this was his book, he would have made a fine story out of Le Mans, 1932. For he also let his ambition run away with him at Arnage, and not only his ambition but his car. He dashed straight into a wood, but seemed unperturbed, and after hacking away the undergrowth continued in the race. Once more Brian Lewis drove magnificently, once more in a Talbot, with which he finished third. He has certainly done all in his power, and the Talbots some of the all in theirs, to reinstate our fallen fortunes. To his English success was added that of the Aston-Martin, which was awarded the Coupe Bienniale.

Before the accustomed fixture of Le Mans, I had entered for an event entirely new to me, and indeed to many Continental drivers. It took place on the Avus track in Berlin; it was preceded by a race for cars of under 1500 c.c., and this was won with the greatest ease by Francis Howe. The next event was for those over 1500 c.c., and had attracted a large entry. But Varzi and Chiron, who were supposed to be taking part, were unable owing to an engagement on the Casablanca track; and in the end I found that I would not be able to race myself. Sir Malcolm Campbell was therefore left alone, but had bad luck with oil trouble in the third lap and was forced to retire. It seemed unlikely that Carraciola would be beaten, but a young driver called von Brauchitsch won from him by a quarter of a mile after a very close race.

On July 10th our peregrinations ended at Francorchamps, for the Belgian Grand Prix d'Endurance. It was won by yet another Alfa-Romeo, who were also second, and, driven by Francis Howe and myself, third. We were about 200 kilometres behind the winner, who covered a record distance.

This year at Brooklands has been a pleasant one for me, though in the Thousand-Mile event, driving with Lord Howe in his own Alfa-Romeo, we retired inconspicuously. But I had at the end of July the best and most exciting race upon that particular track that I can remember. There was a long-standing argument about my single-seater Bentley with its great speed and John Cobb's Delage with its wonderful acceleration. My car had a 4½-litre capacity, and his a 10½ litre; but though we had often been involved in exciting races together, we had never had the course to ourselves. This was now to be granted, and a match like the old horse-racing matches was arranged between the two rivals, the English and the French, for a purse of a hundred sovereigns. At the end of the first lap – the course was over a distance of 8¼ miles, with 3 laps of 2¾ miles each – the Delage led by 3⅘ seconds, as I expected. It's greater acceleration had enabled it to cover a lap from the standing start at 112.17 mph. I tried not to lift my foot once from the accelerator on the next round, and as we went over the famous hump the Bentley gave a terrific heave; but I knew that particular obstacle too well, and John Cobb knew it, too. If he enters an adverse criticism on my criticism of Brooklands I shall have to admit I have been wrong.

On the second lap I caught up, and at the beginning of the third was 1⅖ seconds behind. Gradually I drew nearer the great aluminium Delage, and as we came off the Members' Banking I felt the Bentley, as it were, hang above it for an instant and then shoot ahead. We won by 25 yards or one-fifth of a second, covering the final lap at 137.3 mph. It was a thrilling race, and the long, red single-seater never went better. I can only wish that in all my races there had been so small an entry. But since, in the merry month of May, we were able to beat Kaye Don's lap record by another fifth of a second, and still hold it, it would be ungrateful to end on a note of accusation.

Therefore, for this, the chronological climax, I substitute a note of apology. There are many names that have not adorned these pages as much as their fame deserves. But Time has been against me, and they will know what a potent antagonist he is. Nor have I mentioned at length certain races of undoubted importance, because it has been my object in my limited period to interest rather than instruct; and lest anyone should imagine this to have the air of a conclusion, let me hasten to beg them turn the leaf, and not fall entirely asleep for another four pages.

— CHAPTER XII —

The Course Completed

That is the end. Unleash the hounds of criticism. I am afraid that they will have a great day, ferreting about for misplaced commas, sniffing out errors of technical detail, and finally, when they have run every platitude, illiteracy and solecism to earth, worrying the poor book to death! I have not the official reviewers in mind, whose indulgence I implored at the start; I have already complained that the classic paean of this sport must be penned by the lily-white fingers of poetry, and not by the grimy paw of a mechanic. From the men of letters, therefore, I hope for condescension, if I cannot have approval.

But there must be some people whose acquaintance with cars is adequate to justify expression and from whom I shall get neither. I find every fault magnified, and every condemnation excusable, now that the last page is in print and beyond control; I see that the first chapter was a piece of dishonesty, the second a fanfare of Birkin trumpets, the third only what was expected, the fourth superfluous and rude, the fifth dull racing stories, the sixth will be merely skipped, the seventh more dull racing stories, the eighth, tenth and eleventh more still, the ninth, upstart, pompous and unprovoked, and this last, if it is read, a tedious summary of all the others. I do not know what will be said about me; all I have to say for myself is that I have written the book from love of the sport, and that if people cannot take it at that, they must expect to pay more than seven-and-sixpence. At one point I may have uttered my views too violently, but the subject was so near my own heart and the interest of the country, that I felt I could not underrate its urgency. I have too deep an affection for racing and racing cars, to betray them with weak support; I have too long an experience of them to rant unreasonably.

There is more life and use to this than to any other sport in the world. Rugger and soccer have the speed and many of the thrills, but they do not serve so wide a purpose. Horse-racing has great, but I do not think such great, industrial significance, and cannot exercise the hypnotic beauty of machines. Cricket may become monotonous. Chess is dull.

But motor racing combines so many attractions. It is taken at a pace only exceeded by that of aeroplanes; the spectators watch the long low lines dart by at more than two miles a minute, and feel the wind on their cheeks, and cheer on their favourite lap after lap; the driver answers to the throbbing of the car, and knows that his confidence and eagerness are not misplaced. If he succeeds, he has the cheering and elation that in other sports are seldom concentrated on individuals. He cannot even fail without some sort of excitement, whether it be feverish labour to restart, or a crash that stops his heart a few beats. But there is no fear. There is adventure or confidence. The usual circumstances of life have taught us that disaster is as likely to meet us crossing a street as tearing round a track; in cold blood it is cruel and hideous, but if it comes in the midst of a thrilling race, it is faced with eyes open and a heart not sickened by disease, nor terror, nor suspense. I am sure that de Hane Segrave would not have chosen any other fate than his; it is wrong that those who have met life with courage should at the end be worn down by lingering illness. A man's final appearance is, after all, an outstanding one, and at the outstanding moments he likes to be seen in his true colours. De Hane was fortunate also to die in the one country he never ceased to benefit; the idea of lending his genius elsewhere was repellent. But it was not nearly so often suggested. I doubt what view he would have taken now.

For my poor part, I shall be sorry if I have to go to foreign countries for my racing work and adventures. The English motor crowds, however small and uneducated, have shown themselves always sporting; they have been kind and sympathetic to misfortune, even if they never understood its reason. They know a good driver, and they know a bad driver, nor are they grudging in their applause. I should leave them with the deepest regret, remembering that they once approved of me, and encouraged my driving; but if I ever returned from serving another country, they would show me antagonism without troubling to reason. So I shall strive to remain in England as long as there is any hope of an English car and I shall continue to storm at the people who hinder its creation. I may repeat myself; I may be stuck up in effigy among the ranters of Marble Arch, perched on a wreckage of Alfa-Romeos, and thumping a large British tub. But I shall not cease to thump until somebody listens, even if he does it only out of despair. Should no one listen, then I shall get off that perch and go away to the Continent. There is no reason for anyone to mind my going but it would only occur when the British motor industry was so deep in the mud that I thought nothing in the world could extricate it.

Surely someone must perceive that our surrender would be pitiful. The wings on the Bentley bonnet, formerly those of victory, would seem like the wings of a departed spirit, useless and reproachful. Other countries' advances, by becoming more evident, would make us more ashamed of ourselves, and our hopes and honour be perforce invested in a flock of midgets, whose very great efficiency could never make up for the dead giants; the old green Bentleys would be put under glass cases in museums, and the past few years come to be regarded, as Victorian days by autocratic parents, in the light of a golden era. Perhaps, in a very shorttime, I shall be sitting myself in a deep armchair at my club, mumbling, "Ah, you should have seen us at Le Mans in '29! Those were the days, those were the days!"

Then I shall re-read this book to reinforce my memory, so that it will have had at least one use. Some pictures I remember that nothing can erase; clearest of all I see moments of drama - Sabipa across the road at Pau, with the blood oozing from his head; touches of humour, as George Eyston without his trousers at Montlhéry; then the unresting labours of all my mechanics, and accidents – Chevrollier in flames running past the pits, our crash into the wall at Ballystockart, – and great sportsmen like de Hane Segrave and Nuvolari and Carraciola; and the cars themselves at their birth and at their death. But I always think that I keep the vividest impression of the "Bentley Boys," who seem to have combined in themselves all those many diverse attractions of their sport. They had its courage, its patriotism, its humour, and its adventurous, never bored, never insincere spirit. It is strange how that company has changed in a couple of years. Glen was killed; Clive Dunfee's tragic end still haunts our memory; Babe Barnato has given up motor racing, all the others for one reason or another have disappeared from the road. I believe that I am the only one left who still drives; and now that I am so rarely on an English car, I cannot be taken into account.

I appeal finally to someone, whether he or she has already given aid to a good cause or not, at least to consider this most worthy and remunerative chance. It involves other concerns than cars; it touches the reputation of our country, international friendship, and the relief of unemployment. That motor racing is of the highest importance and in urgent need, I reiterate, giving the dead horse a last beat, to be the conviction of all whose opinions on the matter carry weight. I should be almost glad if this statement met with flat contradiction, and aroused an indignant controversy in the newspapers; there seem very few other ways of bringing it emphatically home to the public. I know there are hundreds who would sell their soul to learn how to drive like an expert, and thousands who ought to be put in prison until they do; but no opportunity is ever given them.

Should the situation ever alter – and at this moment I have heard rumours that it may – I shall not hesitate to leave the Alfa-Romeos and Maseratis where they belong, and put what little experience I have at the right country's disposal. I know that in their heart of hearts the people of England would do their utmost to aid this industry. They have always given their support to the ordinary touring car which they use themselves, and are as exigent of efficiency as any nation on the Continent. Their present disinterest can only be a by-product of the universal depression, and the outcome of a distaste for the very word "industry." I have perhaps been unfair in my accusations; my aid may never have been needed to stimulate them into active assistance. As this book goes to press, they may be planning a great restoration, gathering a wave on the crest of which our motor-racing reputation will return triumphant. Then I shall take a seat in the farthest background, and admit that I have made a storm in a teacup where there was already one in the sky. Then we shall see our road-course built, and our car driven round it. Then, too, the keen and would-be drivers will find the chance to fulfil their ambition. They will learn to gain that confidence which is indispensable, and feel the elation of racing in tune with a perfect car. The diversities of the sport, its jokes and friendships and excitements, will influence them in England, and not among foreigners, however pleasant. Perhaps even they will form a band of their own and revive the days of the "Bentley Boys."

But one thing is certain, that they shall be quite careless of misfortune or disappointment, exhaustion or injury, endeavouring with patience to reach the almost-attainable perfection. Then at length the day will come when they race past the grandstands first, and hear the crowds cheering, and see a little man in a bowler hat let fall the checkered flag, as I let it fall now.

Afterword

We are delighted to be publishing this new edition of Full Throttle by Sir Henry 'Tim' Birkin. Long out of print we have felt for some time that Birkin's classic account of his racing exploits and perspective on motor-racing written nearly 90 years ago deserved a wider audience.

We are very grateful to a number of people who had a hand in helping us achieve his aim. Alan Winn, who was the CEO of Brooklands for 15 years, has kindly written a thoughtful new Foreword for us. He brings a great perspective on what racing those rapid but challenging cars was like, borne of his long experience at Brooklands and enthusiasm for thoroughbred vehicles of the period which includes his 1929 3 litre Bentley that he has owned for over 35 years.

I would like to thank Derek Bell, Great Britain's most successful Le Mans racer and one of the world's top sports car drivers for kindly offering to contribute his reflections on his speedy forbear.

Photographs are an essential component of any Daredevil edition and I would like to thank Diana Spitzley for allowing us to use original Geoffrey Goddard images from the Spitzley/Zagari collection.

We were helpfully directed there by motor racing guru, Doug Nye.

In spite of Coronavirus restrictions, Andrew Lewis at Brooklands was most helpful in sourcing images relating to Birkin and I also appreciate being able to turn to Alex Patterson, also at Brooklands, for his support. Similarly, Jon Day and Patrick Collins of Beaulieu Motor Museum found some lovely photographs for this new edition of 'Full Throttle. We are very fortunate to have these guardians of motor-racing history. Tim Birkin would be amazed if he could look back now at how motor racing has progressed since his day and immensely proud of the times when we have ruled the top echelons of motor sport.

One of the joys of bringing Daredevil Books to life is the wonderfully well-informed and passionate enthusiasts we meet on the journey. I apologise now to them for any unforeseen errors or attributions in the text or photographs that they may spot which we will be happy to correct in future.

Finding an image for the cover that would do the book justice was proving a challenge until I chanced on Paul Dove's wonderful painting of Birkin. It was very generous of him to let us use this image which captures Sir 'Tim' at speed so eloquently and I can recommend his other work.

The text is transferred from the original first edition book but creating a digital file is often fraught with errors so I am very grateful for the proofreading work of my good friend Jo Hall and eagle eyes of my wife in getting the final proofs into shape. I am very fortunate to be married to someone who has far more patience and much better eye for detail than I!

I hope you enjoy this classic book as much as I do. Tim is an engaging and forthright commentator and it is easy to share his delight as he describes hurtling his Bentley at breakneck speed around the racetracks of Europe, for the honour of his team and country.

Toby Hartwell
Daredevil Books 2021

BOSCH
DUNLOP

Reflections

Reflections by Derek Bell MBE,

five times Le Mans Winner

I'm extremely honoured to be asked to write about Sir Henry 'Tim' Birkin, that most speedy and flamboyant member of the famous 'Bentley Boys.' I am flattered to have been asked to add these few words about a sportsman who was without doubt one of the outstanding drivers of that heady period of motor racing.

Birkin was born in 1896 to very successful family lace manufacturing family. He grew up with the Great War approaching and joined the Flying Corps in North Africa; no doubt the excitement of flying aircraft was a stimulus for his desire and passion to race cars. As his subsequent racing career blossomed he married and had three children, all girls. This early period stalled his racing progress, but like all of us, that passion to race and the life surrounding it, the concept of the Bentley Boys and his desire to win Le Mans in an English car sadly took precedence over his family. We have all been there.

He enjoyed the good life, shooting game whenever possible and enjoying sailing in Norfolk with friends. He was a fun-loving man and was liked by all he knew, partying with the Bentley Boys in London, one of the dashing and wealthy young men who could afford the expensive racing game. But he won the admiration of all with his cool skills, fearlessness and sportsmanship on the track.

In 1929 he led a Bentley 1,2,3,4, victory at Le Mans covering 1,770 miles at an average of 74mph, an amazing result for the Boys but in spite of this outstanding success he still wanted to have a car with more power, and speed.

In spite of family concerns over finance he persevered and created his own team in London and worked with Amherst Villiers to develop the Supercharger. It was fitted to the Four and half litre engine in his Bentley as he was adamant he needed the extra horsepower that it would deliver. This was much to W.O.Bentley's dismay, who was a great engineer and had major concerns about its reliability.

The Blower Bentley was born.

Birkin really wanted to win Le Mans in a British car, when no doubt he could have driven for other manufacturers.

In 1930 he led Le Mans with his Blower Bentley

for many hours stretching his car and the Mercedes of Caracciola to both their limits. He retired and soon after the Mercedes followed, worn down by Birkin's blistering pace, giving the Bentley team victory in their own right. So evidently W.O. was correct!

The following year, 1931, Birkin enjoyed his second Le Mans victory when he drove an Alfa Romeo 8C owned by Lord Howe, and was honoured to receive a letter from Mussolini thanking him for his 'winning for Italy'.

Very sadly his life came to a premature end when having driven an Alfa Romeo into 3rd in the Tripoli GP in 1933, he burnt his arm on the exhaust of his Maserati; but he took little notice of it, his burns became infected and he passed away three weeks later. What an unfortunate way to die, but treatment wasn't what it is today.

Birkin was sadly missed; a passionate advocate of Great Britain taking motor racing seriously. Incredibly fast in any car he drove he was a true sportsman and much admired-hero of the time.

I believe the fact that there was a well-attended celebration of his life at his favourite place, Blakeney in Norfolk where he is buried, some 60 years later says it all about the continued respect the motoring world have for this exceptional man.

Milton Keynes UK
Ingram Content Group UK Ltd.
UKHW011502170624
444324UK00038B/503

9 781913 568696